MCWP 2-22
(formerly MCWP 2-15.2)

I0416456

Signals Intelligence

U.S. Marine Corps

PCN 14300006300

MCCDC (C 42)
13 Jul 2004

E R R A T U M

to

MCWP 2-22

SIGNALS INTELLIGENCE

1. Change the publication short title to read "MCWP 2-22" (vice MCWP 2-15.2).

PCN 143 000063 80

DEPARTMENT OF THE NAVY
Headquarters United States Marine Corps
Washington, D.C. 20380-1775

22 February 1999

FOREWORD

Marine Corps Warfighting Publication (MCWP) 2-22, *Signals Intelligence*, serves as a basic reference for understanding concepts, operations, and procedures for the conduct of signals intelligence (SIGINT) operations in support of the Marine air-ground task force. This publication complements and expands on Marine Corps Doctrinal Publication 2, *Intelligence*, and MCWP 2-1, *Intelligence Operations,* which provide doctrine and higher order tactics, techniques, and procedures for intelligence operations.

The primary target audience of this publication is intelligence personnel responsible for planning and executing SIGINT operations. Personnel who provide support to SIGINT or who use the results from these operations should also read this publication.

MCWP 2-22 describes aspects of SIGINT operations, including doctrinal fundamentals, equipment, command and control, communications and information systems support, planning, execution, security, and training. Detailed information on SIGINT operations and tactics, techniques, and procedures is classified and beyond the scope of this publication.

MCWP 2-22 supersedes Fleet Marine Force Manual 3-23, (C) *Signals Intelligence/Electronic Warfare Operations* (U), dated 21 September 1990.

Reviewed and approved this date.

BY DIRECTION OF THE COMMANDANT OF THE MARINE CORPS

J. E. RHODES
Lieutenant General, U.S. Marine Corps
Commanding General
Marine Corps Combat Development Command

DISTRIBUTION: 143 000063 00

To Our Readers

Changes: Readers of this publication are encouraged to submit suggestions and changes that will improve it. Recommendations may be sent directly to Commanding General, Marine Corps Combat Development Command, Doctrine Division (C 42), 3300 Russell Road, Suite 318A, Quantico, VA 22134-5021 or by fax to 703-784-2917 (DSN 278-2917) or by E-mail to **smb@doctrine div@mccdc**. Recommendations should include the following information:

- Location of change
  Publication number and title
  Current page number
  Paragraph number (if applicable)
  Line number
  Figure or table number (if applicable)
- Nature of change
  Add, delete
  Proposed new text, preferably double-spaced and typewritten
- Justification and/or source of change

Additional copies: A printed copy of this publication may be obtained from Marine Corps Logistics Base, Albany, GA 31704-5001, by following the instructions in MCBul 5600, *Marine Corps Doctrinal Publications Status.* An electronic copy may be obtained from the Doctrine Division, MCCDC, world wide web home page which is found at the following universal reference locator: **http://www.doctrine.quantico.usmc.mil**.

Unless otherwise stated, whenever the masculine or feminine gender is used,
both men and women are included.

Signals Intelligence

Table of Contents

		Page
Chapter 1.	**Fundamentals**	
1001	What is Signals Intelligence?	1-1
1002	Concept of Employment	1-1
1003	SIGINT and Electronic Warfare	1-2
1004	Threats	1-3
1005	All-Source Intelligence and Operations Command Support	1-3
1006	Capabilities	1-4
1007	Limitations	1-5
1008	Organization	1-5
1009	Command and Control	1-6
1010	Operations	1-6
1011	Commanders' Responsibilities	1-8
Chapter 2.	**SIGINT Responsibilities in the Supporting Establishment**	
2001	Marine Corps SIGINT Organization	2-1
2002	SIGINT Organizations in Other Military Services	2-2
2003	National SIGINT Organizations	2-3
Chapter 3.	**SIGINT Responsibilities in the MAGTF**	
3001	Commanders, Marine Corps Forces	3-1
3002	MAGTF Staff Sections	3-1
3003	MAGTF Intelligence Section Elements	3-2
3004	Marine Divisions and Aircraft Wings	3-5
3005	Radio Battalions	3-5
3006	VMAQs	3-5
Chapter 4.	**Radio Battalion**	
4001	Tasks	4-1
4002	Organization	4-1
4003	Task Organization for MAGTF Operations SIGINT Support Unit	4-3
4004	Command and Control	4-5
4005	Notional Concepts of Employment and Task Organizations	4-5

Chapter 5. Marine Tactical Electronic Warfare Squadrons

5001	Mission and Tasks	5-1
5002	Organization and Concept of Employment	5-1
5003	EA-6B Prowler	5-2
5004	Tactical EA-6B Mission Planning System	5-4
5005	TERPES	5-4

Chapter 6. Communications and Information Systems

6001	Basic MAGTF SIGINT CIS Requirements	6-1
6002	Notional MAGTF SIGINT Operational Architectures	6-2
6003	Planning Consideration	6-7
6004	SIGINT Communications	6-7

Chapter 7. Planning and Operations

| Section I | SIGINT Functional Planning | 7-1 |

7101	SIGINT Concept of Operations	7-1
7102	Enemy Characteristics	7-1
7103	Topography	7-2
7104	Planning Responsibilities	7-3
7105	Coordination of SIGINT Operations	7-3

| Section II | SIGINT Operational Planning | 7-5 |

7201	Planning and Direction	7-5
7202	Collection	7-6
7203	Processing and Exploitation	7-7
7204	Production	7-8
7205	Dissemination	7-8
7206	Utilization	7-10

| Section III | SIGINT Plans and Orders | 7-11 |

| Section IV | Execution | 7-12 |

Chapter 8. Security of Sensitive Compartmented Information

8001	Special Security Officer	8-2
8002	Personnel Security Program	8-2
8003	Physical Security	8-3
8004	Information Systems Security	8-5

Chapter 9.   Training

9001	Military Occupational Specialty Training	9-1
9002	Functional Training	9-2
9003	Exercises	9-2
9004	Operational Training Objectives	9-3

Appendices

A	Radio Battalion SIGINT Support Unit Checklist	A-1
B	Marine Corps SIGINT Equipment	B-1
C	SIGINT and SCI Security Management Operations Flowchart	C-1
D	SIGINT Appendix Format	D-1
E	TSCIF Checklist	E-1
F	Glossary	F-1
G	References and Related Publications	G-1

List of Figures

1-1	The Intelligence Cycle	1-7
4-1	Radio Battalion Organization	4-2
4-2	SIGINT Support Unit Elements	4-3
4-3	Notional SSU Fly-In Echelon Configuration	4-6
5-1	EA-6B Prowler	5-2
5-2	VMAQ Organization	5-2
5-3	VMAQ and TERPES Operations	5-3
6-1	Notional MEF SIGINT Operational Architecture	6-3
6-2	Notional MEF Lead Echelon SIGINT Operational Architecture	6-4
6-3	MEU(SOC) CE Afloat SIGINT Operational Architecture	6-5
6-4	MEU(SOC) CE Ashore SIGINT Operational Architecture	6-6
6-5	MEF CE CIC Communications and Information Systems Architecture	6-9
6-6	RadBn SSU Operations Control and Analysis Center Communications and Information Systems	6-10
6-7	VMAQ Operations Center and TERPES Communications and Information Systems	6-11
7-1	MAGTF and Supporting SIGINT Operations	7-13
B-1	AN/ULQ-19(V2)	B-1
B-2	AN/MLQ-36	B-2
B-3	AN/MLQ-36A	B-3
B-4	AN/PRD-12	B-4
B-5	AN/MSC-63A	B-5
B-6	AN/MSC-63A (interior view)	B-5
B-7	Technical Control and Analysis Center Concept of Employment	B-6
B-8	Team Portable Collection System Upgrade	B-8

B-9	Team Portable Collection System COMINT Collection Subsystem	B-8
B-10	Team Portable Collection System Analysis Subsystem	B-9
B-11	Trojan Spirit II	B-10
B-12	RREP SS-1	B-11
B-13	RREP SS-2	B-11
B-14	Rifle-Mounted HIDRAH	B-12
B-15	EA-6B Prowler	B-14
B-16	AN/TSQ-90D/E(V), TERPES Portable Unit	B-14

List of Tables

2-1	Marine Support Battalion Companies	2-2
4-1	Notional MEU(SOC) SSU T/O	4-7
4-2	Notional Fly-In Echelon T/O	4-7
7-1	Emitter Technical Data	7-2

Chapter 1

Fundamentals

All military forces use the electromagnetic spectrum to command and control operating forces acquire targets, guide weapons, and direct supporting arms. These military forces also use the electromagnetic spectrum to collect, process, and report intelligence and to support other administrative and logistics operations. Most facets o military operations involve the use of some device or system that radiates or receives electromagnetic energy via air waves, metallic cable, or fiber optics. Radios, radars, sensors, smart munitions, telephone systems, and computer networks use electromagnetic radiation. Both complex and unsophisticated military organizations depend on these systems and their inherent use of the electromagnetic spectrum. Signals intelligence operations are the principal way to exploit an adversary's use of the electromagnetic spectrum.

1001. What Is Signals Intelligence?

Signals intelligence (SIGINT) is "a category o intelligence comprising either individually or in combination all communications intelligence, electronic intelligence, and foreign instrumentation signals intelligence, however transmitted" (Joint Pub 1-02). Simply, SIGINT is intelligence gained by exploiting an adversary's use of the electromagnetic spectrum with the aim of gaining undetected firsthand intelligence on the adversary's intentions, dispositions, capabilities, and limitations.

a. Communications Intelligence

Communications intelligence (COMINT) is the technical and intelligence information derived from foreign communications by anyone othe than the intended recipient.

b. Electronics Intelligence

Electronics intelligence (ELINT) is the technical and intelligence information derived from foreign noncommunication electromagnetic radiation emanating from anywhere other than nuclear detonations or radioactive sources.

c. Foreign Instrumentation Signals Intelligence

Foreign instrumentation signals intelligence (FISINT) is the technical and intelligence information derived from the intercept of foreign instrumentation signals by anyone other than the intended recipients. (FISINT is primarily strategic in nature and will not be addressed further in this manual.)

1002. Concept of Employment

SIGINT can be employed in tactical situation when the enemy uses electromagnetic spectru communications and/or systems. Optimal employment is against enemy forces that depend on tactical communications and noncommunications for command and control of their operations. SIGINT operations are more difficult against enemy forces that have established more permanent emplacements using land lines or other cabled communications systems.

SIGINT is one of several intelligence disciplines. The other key intelligence disciplines are imagery intelligence (IMINT), human resources intelligence (HUMINT), and measurement and signature intelligence (MASINT).

1003. SIGINT and Electronic Warfare

Electronic warfare (EW) is "any military action involving the use of electromagnetic and directed energy to control the electromagnetic spectrum or to attack the enemy" (Joint Pub 1-02). EW denies the enemy use of the electromagnetic spectru for command and control and protects it for friendly command and control. There are three divisions of EW.

a. Electronic Warfare Support

Electronic warfare support (ES) includes actions tasked by or under the direct control of an operational commander to search for, intercept, identify, and locate sources of intentional and unintentional radiated enemy electromagnetic signals for the purpose of *immediate* threat recognition. ES provides information required for immediate tactical decisions and operations such as the identification of imminent hostile actions, threat avoidance, targeting, or electronic attack.

Both SIGINT and ES involve searching for, intercepting, identifying, and locating electronic emitters. The primary differences between the two are the information's intended use, the degree of analytical effort expended, the detail of information provided, and the timeliness required.

SIGINT is used to gain information concerning the enemy, usually in response to a priority intelligence requirement (PIR), an intelligence requirement (IR), or other means. As described in chapter 6, SIGINT support is usually provided to the Marine air-ground task force (MAGTF) as a whole, but may also be provided directly to subordinate elements.

SIGINT information is normally provided to the MAGTF all-source fusion center (AFC) for inclusion into all-source intelligence products and for further dissemination throughout the MAGTF and to external organizations. See Marine Corps Warfighting Publication [MCWP] 2-1, *Intelligence Operations*. SIGINT-derived information of immediate tactical importance that does not re-

quire further processing, correlation, or analysi may be passed directly to subordinate commanders or to the operations section or supporting arms element of supported commands, in accordance with United States Signals Intelligence Directive (USSID) 316, *Non-Codeword Reporting Program*, and USSID 240, *ELINT Processing, Analysis, Reporting, and Forwarding Procedures*.

b. Electronic Attack

Electronic attack (EA) is action taken to prevent or reduce an enemy's effective use of the electromagnetic spectrum.

The objectives of SIGINT may conflict with those of EA. For example, EA may be conducted to interfere with the adversary's use of an emitter a the same time as SIGINT operations are designed to exploit the adversary's use of the same emitter. Furthermore, EA operations against one target may disrupt or otherwise interfere with friendly SIGINT collection against the same or differen targets.

SIGINT operations, EA operations, and the MAGTF's overall use of the electromagnetic spectrum for command and control (C2) operations must be carefully coordinated within the MAGTF and with pertinent external organizations. Depending on operational requirements, SIGINT and EA operations coordination and deconfliction may occur within the radio battalion operations control and analysis center (OCAC) within the electronic warfare coordination center (EWCC), or within the MAGTF command element (CE) current operations center (COC).

c. Electronic Protection

Electronic protection (EP) involves the action taken to ensure effective, friendly use of the electromagnetic spectrum despite the enemy's use of EW. Within the MAGTF, SIGINT elements may be tasked to employ similar techniques agains friendly force electronic emitters in order to identify and help eliminate signals security vulnerabilities that could be exploited by an enemy's SIGINT operations.

1004. Threats

a. Enemy Capabilities

The more a combat unit relies on the electromagnetic spectrum, the more vulnerable it is to the enemy's signals intelligence and electronic warfare actions. The enemy can—

- Detect a unit's devices which radiate electromagnetic energy to reveal its identity and location.

- Monitor a unit's communications to reveal its intentions, combat capabilities, logistics and personnel status, and other critical operational and tactical information.

- Inject false information into communications and information systems (CIS) to confuse and mislead a unit.

- Interrupt a unit's use of the electromagnetic spectrum, thereby degrading its ability to receive and process intelligence, plan operations, and execute C2 functions.

b. Countermeasures

To counter threats listed and to enhance effectiveness, Marines must be able to—

- Protect, to the maximum extent possible, the free use of the electromagnetic spectrum and ensure the reliable performance of ou CIS.

- Exploit the enemy's use of the electromagnetic spectrum for intelligence and targeting and intrude into the enemy's CIS and networks.

- Attack the enemy's CIS to adversely affect their decisionmaking process and operations.

1005. All-Source Intelligence and Operations Command Support

Generally, SIGINT is more useful to the commander and the decisionmaking process when has been correlated and fused with information from other intelligence sources and disseminated in easily usable, tailored, all-source intelligence products. Tactical SIGINT operations within the MAGTF, along with other services, theater, and national SIGINT support, make SIGINT a valuable source of information within the overall intelligence effort. SIGINT supports the following six functions of intelligence.

a. Commander's Estimate

SIGINT helps formulate and modify the commander's estimate of the situation by providing information needed to analyze the enemy's C2 operations, identify the current parameters of operating emitters, give insight into enemy intentions, and assess the enemy's intelligence, EW and other military capabilities.

b. Development of the Situation

SIGINT's ability to track enemy emitters and associated units and to obtain indicators of intentions can confirm or refute potential enemy courses of action. SIGINT also helps commanders to better understand the enemy and the battlespace, thereby reducing uncertainty by acquiring information regarding enemy structure, dispositions, locations, movements, and operational activities and patterns.

c. Indications and Warning

SIGINT is often the principal provider of indications and warning (I&W) because adversaries often reveal their intentions, locations, and movements in their communications and other electronic emissions.

d. Force Protection

SIGINT supports force protection by revealing critical intelligence about enemy intelligence, sabotage, subversion, and terrorism and by assessing the vulnerability of friendly C2 and CI operations.

e. Targeting

SIGINT supports targeting by providing key operational and locational intelligence on enemy C2 operations and facilities, weapons systems, force compositions, and dispositions. Information provided through SIGINT can identify high value and high payoff targets and help develop options for attacking these targets. SIGINT also supports all-source intelligence gain and loss assessments of potential enemy targets.

f. Combat Assessment

SIGINT can aid in all-source intelligence support of battle damage assessments by exploiting enemy reports of sustained battle damages and by detecting changes in enemy operations subsequen to friendly attacks.

1006. Capabilities

a. Remote Intelligence

SIGINT operations provide extended-range intelligence without the need for physical presence within or near the surveillance area. The standoff range for SIGINT operations is directly dependent on the characteristics of the terrain in which SIGINT collection is being conducted and the type, operating characteristics, and methods of employment of the enemy's electromagnetic systems. Some enemy electromagnetic systems may require that SIGINT operations be close to the transmission origin, path, or medium. Conversely, other electromagnetic systems may be exploitable from positions farther away from the transmission origin, path, or medium.

(1) Ground SIGINT Elements. Locating ground SIGINT operational elements with friendly combat forces provides the friendly commander with the capability to collect a wide range of intelligence information. Locating SIGINT element with the ground combat element (GCE) forces provides the MAGTF commander with intelligence support for decisionmaking as well as I&W and force protection intelligence reporting to the local unit.

(2) Air-Platform SIGINT Elements. Airborn SIGINT elements can provide direct support to both air and ground operations and significantly enhance collection operations by exploiting enemy targets masked or otherwise unattainable by ground-based elements. These SIGINT elements also support friendly air operations by identifying, locating, and determining the status of enemy surveillance, targeting, and weapons systems and by providing intelligence support to friendly EA operations targeting these enemy systems.

(3) Ship-Based SIGINT Elements. SIGINT elements may operate from ship-based SIGIN operations facilities in support of amphibious operations. Marine and Navy elements operating from ship-based SIGINT facilities may support amphibious operations as a part of the assault force, airborne SIGINT operations, or ship-based SIGINT operations. Within an amphibious task force (ATF), the principal SIGINT facilities are found with ship's signals exploitation spaces (SSESs) located within the intelligence centers of many ships.

b. Target Detection and Identification

SIGINT can detect enemy activity in designated areas and provide a general indication of its type and volume. Analysis of SIGINT information can provide the identity and location of specific enemy units, indications of enemy plans and future operations, and the type, function, and location of specific enemy units and systems.

c. Near-Real-Time Reporting

SIGINT operations can immediately report enemy actions or events critical to the operations of friendly units. Time-sensitive SIGINT reporting to combat units may be via standard MAGTF intelligence communications channels or any available direct communications means.

d. Continuous Operations

SIGINT operations are conducted on a 24-hou basis. The size and composition of SIGINT forces along with the supported commander(s)'s concept of operations will influence the scope, services and capabilities of SIGINT operations.

e. Stealth

SIGINT operations are a passive intelligence technique and can usually be conducted withou the enemy's knowledge or detection. EW operations include both active and passive techniques and, depending on implementation, may or may not be recognized by the enemy.

f. Flexibility

Marine SIGINT operations may be employed in a variety of means to support the MAGTF concept of operations and supporting intelligence operations. SIGINT elements may be deployed with advance forces or forward ground units; they may be aboard air platforms or ship-based. Additionally, Marine SIGINT elements routinely operate with joint and other service elements. These elements are effective at leveraging their capabilities in support of MAGTF requirements.

1007. Limitations

a. Enemy System

The primary value of SIGINT operations is against enemy systems using electromagnetic spectrum system transmissions. SIGINT operations are ineffective against systems that do no use radio frequency (RF) transmissions (e.g., fiber optics, land-line telephone systems, or other cabled systems). If the enemy conducts operations under enemy emission control (EMCON) conditions (e.g., radio silence), SIGINT operations will not be effective.

b. Terrain Masking

Heavily wooded and urban areas reduce the susceptibility of enemy transmissions to SIGINT collection. In these areas, generally, SIGINT elements must be closer to the enemy's transmission origin or medium. Mountainous or very hilly terrain also inhibits SIGINT operations (particularly ground-based operations) by effectively blocking enemy signals from detection.

c. Complex Signals

Enemy signals that are complex or encrypted reduce the intelligence information available from the transmission. Complex signals (i.e., frequency hoppers) require special equipment for intercep and signals analysis. Encrypted signals require deciphering to reveal intelligence information. Deciphering simple encryption methods may be possible, but an enemy's use of complex encryption methods is currently beyond the scope of tactical SIGINT elements.

d. SIGINT versus Electronic Attack

SIGINT operations may be affected when enemy signals are being jammed. Prior to initiating EA jamming operations, consideration must be given to the intelligence value of the enemy's signal and the effects of its loss.

1008. Organization

Within the Marine Corps, the units responsible for the conduct of tactical SIGINT are the two radio battalions and the four Marine tactical electronic warfare squadrons.

a. Radio Battalion

The radio battalion (RadBn) provides tactical SIGINT, electronic warfare, communications security monitoring and analysis, and special communications operations in support of the MAGTF. A variety of employment concepts may be used depending upon the situation. Refer to chapter 4 for a detailed description of RadBns.

b. Marine Tactical Electronic Warfare Squadron

The Marine tactical electronic warfare squadron (VMAQ) conducts tactical electronic reconnaissance and ELINT operations in support of the MAGTF.

The VMAQ provides—

- ELINT collection operations to maintain the electronic order of battle, including identification of selected emitters and location o nonfriendly emitters.
- Threat warnings for friendly aircraft, ships, and ground units.
- Intelligence support to prevent, delay, or interrupt detection and tracking by enemy early warning, acquisition, and fire or missile control radars of aviation combat elemen (ACE) operations and Marine EA-6B tacti cal jamming aircraft in support of strike aircraft.

Refer to chapter 5 for a detailed description of the VMAQ.

1009. Command and Control

a. Radio Battalion

The RadBn (or RadBn detachment) is generally a subordinate command of, or attached to, the MAGTF CE. The MAGTF commander has operational control (OPCON) of the RadBn (or RadBn detachment).

(1) Staff Cognizance. The MAGTF commander exercises C2 over the RadBn or its detachments via the MAGTF intelligence officer. Such a relationship allows for the centralized direction and effective integration of SIGINT operations within the MAGTF's broader all-source intelligence concept of operations. RadBn's EW operations fa under the staff cognizance of the MAGTF operations officer, requiring close coordination and integration among the intelligence staff officer (G-2/S-2), operations staff officer (G-3/S-3), and

communications and information systems officer (G-6/S-6) to achieve optimum employment of RadBn.

(2) Support Relationships The RadBn most typically operates in general support of the MAGTF. However, RadBn or its elements may be employed in direct support of any of the MAGTF's major support elements, i.e., GCE and ACE. In such cases, the scope of the supported commander's control over assigned RadBn elements usually is specified to ensure effective support of operations while allowing the MAGTF commander to maintain effective control of broader intelligence and SIGINT operations.

b. Marine Tactical Electronic Warfare Squadron

VMAQ or its detachments are subordinate to the ACE and under the OPCON of the ACE commander.

(1) Staff Cognizance. The ACE commander will usually exercise C2 over VMAQ via the ACE operations officer or tactical air command center (TACC). The ACE intelligence officer will exercise staff cognizance over VMAQ ELINT activities beyond that required to support EA missions.

(2) Support Relationships. VMAQ elements principally operate in direct support of ACE operations or other designated commanders (e.g., the joint force air component commander). However, ELINT acquired during VMAQ operations is capable of being used in general support of MAGTF elements and supporting intelligence operations.

1010. Operations

RadBn and VMAQ conduct both COMINT and ELINT operations to varying degrees. RadBns conduct predominantly COMINT operations; they also ensure rapid dissemination of fused ELIN and COMINT from organic or external sources to the G-2/S-2 and subordinate commanders. The VMAQ's main focus is ELINT and ES.

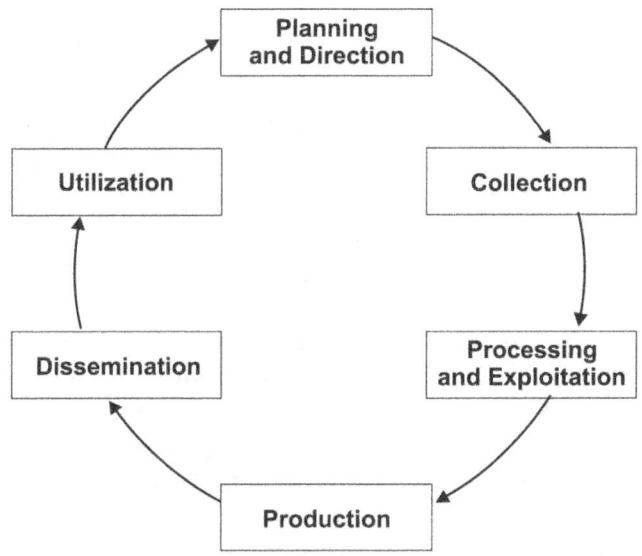

Figure 1-1. The Intelligence Cycle.

To complete intelligence tasks, RadBn an VMAQ incorporate the six intelligence cycle phases into their SIGINT methodology (see figure 1-1). Products of the SIGINT cycle are disseminated to commanders and others through the MAGTF intelligence officer. RadBn and VMAQ also provide SIGINT products to other Service and agencies as directed.

a. Planning and Direction

SIGINT direction is a continuous process that encompasses the tactical and technical employment of SIGINT assets. It begins on receipt of a warning order, initiating directive, or establishment of a planning objective and continues until termination of the mission. SIGINT unit commanders closely coordinate their operations with the MAGTF intelligence officer and pertinent external intelligence and SIGINT elements.

Planning and direction involves—

- Determining PIR and IR and SIGINT requirements to support them.
- Preparing supporting SIGINT collection, production, and dissemination plans.
- Issuing orders and requests to SIGINT units.
- Checking continuously on the productivity and effectiveness of SIGINT collectors, pro-

ducers, disseminators, and other SIGINT elements and agencies.

b. Collection

During collection, organic, attached, and supporting SIGINT elements detect, collect, and record COMINT and ELINT data. The collected COMINT and ELINT data is then delivered to the appropriate SIGINT processing or production element. The OCAC is the processing and production element for RadBn, while the Tactical Electronic Reconnaissance Processing and Evaluation System (TERPES) is VMAQ's processing and production element. In some instances, such as immediate threat information, PIRs and supporting reporting criteria may direct the SIGINT collector to disseminate SIGINT reports directly to the local commander (e.g., an infantry maneuver element) for immediate support to operations.

c. Processing and Exploitation

SIGINT processing consists of converting and formatting raw signals data to a form that is usable in follow-on SIGINT and all-source intelligence analysis. The processing and exploitation phase is usually not a discrete function, but rather one that is accomplished during collection. Once the collected information has been processed, analysis must determine its significance. Other intelligence information may also be fused together with the processed SIGINT to give a comprehensive picture and to show how the information can be used by the commander to gain an advantage.

d. Production

The production stage involves converting the SIGINT analysis into appropriately tailored SIGINT reports and all-source intelligence product that can be easily understood by the commander and other users. Specifically formatted standardized messages, graphics, and other intelligence products are required to familiarize these user with layout and content and to ensure rapid usage and automated processing of finished reports. Within the MAGTF, the RadBn OCAC and the VMAQ TERPES produce SIGINT reports and products, and the MAGTF AFC incorporates

SIGINT products and information into all-source intelligence products.

e. Dissemination

Dissemination is the process through which SIGINT products are delivered to MAGTF users: the MAGTF commander, subordinate commanders and their staffs, and others as appropriate (e.g. joint force commander, joint components, and various theater and national organizations and intelligence agencies). SIGINT products are disseminated via dedicated SIGINT or general purpose CIS channels according to available CIS resources, the classification of the product, and the intelligence dissemination plan. These products include time-sensitive voice reports, text reports, data base updates, and web-based resources (e.g., via the MAGTF sensitive compartmented information local area network).

f. Utilization

SIGINT must be exploited to have value. Commanders, G-2/S-2s, G-3/S-3s, and other principal staff officers must continuously evaluate SIGINT products for timeliness, usefulness, and overa quality and provide feedback to the intelligence officer and SIGINT elements.

1011. Commanders' Responsibilities

MAGTF commanders are responsible for the planning and direction, collection, processing production, dissemination, utilization, and security of all SIGINT information by units under their command. The Director, National Security Agency (DIRNSA), delegates SIGINT operational tasking authority (SOTA) to MAGTF commanders by name for the duration of an operation o other specified period of time. SOTA allows the designated commander to task and direct the operations of organic or attached SIGINT units. Additional information regarding SOTA may be found in USSID 4, *Concept of SIGINT Support to Military Commanders*.

Commanders are also responsible for planning integrating, and using SIGINT support, if available, from other United States or allied nationa and military SIGINT organizations. The commander's primary responsibilities fall into the following areas.

a. Tasking and Directing

The commander possessing SOTA is responsible for the effective tasking and operation of assigned SIGINT assets. Generally, once a commander determines the intelligence requirements, the G-2 S-2, with the advice and assistance of the intelligence operations officer and SIGINT officer (SIO), decides which requirements can be satisfied via organic SIGINT operations. SIGINT unit commanders or officers in charge (OICs) will also coordinate operations with other key staff officers within the intelligence section (i.e., the collections manager, the AFC OIC, the surveillance and reconnaissance center OIC, and the dissemination manager). The G-2/S-2 passes these IRs as taskings to the commanding officer (CO) or OIC o the organic or attached SIGINT unit (e.g., a RadBn unit). These requirements will be in the form of either PIRs or IRs. PIRs and IRs are further managed within the intelligence effor through the use of intelligence collection requirements (ICRs), intelligence production requirements (IPRs), and intelligence dissemination requirements (IDRs) in order to achieve effective, mutually supporting all-source intelligence operations (see MCWP 2-1, chapter 3, for detailed information on IR management). The SIGINT unit commander is then responsible for commanding and controlling resources to accomplish the assigned mission. This process is discussed further in chapter 7.

b. Reporting

The ultimate goal of tactical SIGINT operations is the timely and usable production of SIGINT information which answers the MAGTF commander's PIRs and other MAGTF IRs. SIGINT reports are discussed in detail in chapter 7.

c. Protecting

The MAGTF commander is responsible for safeguarding SIGINT personnel, facilities, and information used or produced by units within the command. Loss of SIGINT units and capabilities by destruction or capture and unintended disclosures of SIGINT operations may result in severe losses of MAGTF capabilities. The effectiveness of SIGINT depends on the ability to maintain security and conceal SIGINT techniques and success from the adversary. Accordingly, the commander must provide adequate protection to prevent the capture of SIGINT facilities and personnel. In addition, special intelligence courier must be adequately protected, and positive measures must be taken to conceal courier runs and routes. To meet this responsibility, the MAGT commander must satisfy the following four basi security requirements.

(1) A special security officer (SSO) must be appointed in all units authorized to receive and use SCI. The SSO is under the staff cognizance of the unit intelligence officer and is responsible for the operation of the SCIF and the security, control, and use of SCI within the SCIF. Marine expeditionary force (MEF) CEs, Marine divisions, Marine aircraft wings, force service support groups, and other designated organizations have SSOs. Other SSOs may also be appointed as needed during tactical operations or whenever a TSCIF is established.

(2) Sensitive compartmented information (SCI generally must be handled, processed, or stored only in a SCI facility (SCIF). This may be either a mobile tactical SCIF (TSCIF) or a permanent facility. SCI security requirements are discussed in greater detail in chapter 8.

(3) Persons who handle or use SIGINT information must have proper security clearances and be indoctrinated for access to SCI and any additional required accesses. Access to SCI will be governed by need-to-know requirements. Unit commanders are responsible for determining who requires SCI access. At a minimum, all unit staff principals and key functional planners should have SCI access.

(4) SCI-secure CIS means for handling and transmitting special intelligence and SIGINT-related information must be available. These include SCI voice circuits, SCI record communications, SC local area networks (LANs), and Joint Worldwide Intelligence Communications System (JWICS).

d. Training

The MAGTF commander is responsible for ensuring that staff and operating forces are trained to effectively use SIGINT and to protect themselves against enemy SIGINT efforts.

Chapter 2

SIGINT Responsibilities in the Supporting Establishment

RadBns and VMAQs are the principal SIGINT units within the operating forces. These units are addressed further in chapters 4 and 5. To effectively execute their missions, MAGTFs, RadBns, and VMAQs draw on a wide range of external organizations to provide personnel and equipmen resources, training opportunities, and unique SIGINT support. To understand how MAGTF SIGINT operations can be supported externally, it is necessary to understand the missions and functions of external SIGINT organizations and how they provide operational support to the MAGTF.

2001. Marine Corps SIGINT Organization

a. Headquarters Marine Corps

Headquarters Marine Corps (HQMC) is responsible for the internal organization, training, equipping, and readiness of the Marine Corps; for the operation of its material support system; and for the total performance of the Marine Corps. The Assistant Chief of Staff, Command, Control, Communications, Computers, and Intelligence Department (C4I), has the following SIGINT responsibilities:

- Formulates Marine Corps SIGINT plans and policies and participates in the formulation of joint and combined plans, policies, and related command relationships.

- Determines present and future SIGINT active and reserve personnel requirements, both quantitative and qualitative.

- Provides final authority on validation and approval of all personnel augmentation from non-Fleet Marine Force (FMF) resources to support MAGTF operations.

- Reviews the internal organization, training requirements, and readiness of all SIGIN elements of the Marine Corps. The internal organization of Marine Corps SIGINT elements is constantly reviewed, with particular emphasis on occupational field (OccFld) military occupational specialty (MOS) skill requirements, to ensure requisite skills and training are available to meet MAGTF operational needs.

b. Marine Support Battalion

The Marine support battalion (MarSptBn) is a special supporting activity that provides for Marine Corps participation in national and Department of the Navy (DON) cryptologic activities. (SIGINT operations within the Navy are generally referred to as *cryptologic* operations This term may generally be used synonymously with the term *SIGINT*.) Marines in MarSptBn are assigned to national and theater organizations that support both deployed and in-garrison MAGTFs with routine and time-sensitive, mission-critica SIGINT support. Additionally, these Marines learn national-level SIGINT collection, production, and dissemination systems and benefit from SIGINT skills training available only at these sites.

(1) Commanding Officer. The principal functions and tasks assigned to the CO, MarSptBn, include the following:

- Coordinate the withdrawal of MarSptBn Marines to augment MAGTFs in response to global-sourcing requests.

- Support Marine Corps SIGINT requirements through interface at the National Security Operations Center (NSOC) and regional security operations centers

(RSOCs). (Refer to paragraph 2003 for a detailed discussion of these organizations.)

- Manage and administer the reserve SIGINT program to provide augmentation to active duty SIGINT forces.

- Provide for entry-level skills qualification and skills progression training of Marine SIGINT personnel.

(2) Battalion Headquarters. The battalion headquarters, collocated with Commander, Naval Security Group (CNSG), Fort Meade, Maryland, provides command, administrative, and Marine Corps-unique logistics support for the battalion and Marine Corps personnel in various Naval Security Group (NSG). It is under the military command and management control of the Commandant of the Marine Corps (CMC) and under the staff cognizance of the Assistant Chief of Staff, C4I, HQMC.

(3) Letter Companies. MarSptBn's letter companies support the naval mission of the Naval Security Group Activity (NSGA) to which they are assigned as well as provide for the unique service support of assigned Marines (see table 2-1). The letter companies are under the military command and administrative control of the CO, MarSptBn, while under the OPCON and technical direction of the CO of the NSGA site each supports.

(4) Company K. Company K, MarSptBn, provides administration for Marine students and staff assigned to the Naval Technological Training Center (NTTC), Pensacola, Florida, and provides liaison and instructors in conjunction with SIGINT training.

2002. SIGINT Organizations in Other Military Services

Services man, train, and equip organic SIGIN forces to support their operational commander and to prepare to participate in joint, theater, national, and combined operations. Each Service has a service cryptologic element (SCE) headquarters that provides SIGINT management, guidance, and oversight. The National Security Agency (NSA) maintains SIGINT operational control of each SCE.

Table 2-1. Marine Support Battalion Companies.

Company	Site/Host	Location
Headquarters Company	NSG	Ft. Meade, Maryland
Company A	NSGA Denver	Buckley Air National Guard Base, Aurora, Colorad
Company B	NSG	Ft. Meade, Maryland
Company D	NSGA Ft. Gordon	Ft. Gordon, Georgia
Company E	NSGA Misawa	Misawa Air Force Base (AFB), Japan
Company F[1]	NSGA Rota	Rota, Spain
Company G	NSGA Menwith Hill	Royal Air Force Menwith Hill, England
Company H	NSGA San Antonio	Kelly AFB, San Antonio, Texas
Company I	NSGA Kunia	Kunia, Hawaii
Company K	NTTC Corry Station	Pensacola, Florida
Company L	NSGA Guantanamo	Guantanamo Bay, Cuba
[1]Company F is scheduled for deactivation 30 June 1999.		

a. Naval Security Group

NSG is the DON's SCE. It directly supports deployed MAGTFs by providing access to—

- SSES use with MAGTF SIGINT personnel while embarked.
- Direct support to MAGTF operations with NSG elements operating aboard Navy ships or aircraft.
- Direct service support to MAGTF operations from ashore NSG facilities in the theater of operations.
- Hardware, software, specialized equipment, and training to the RadBns.
- SIGINT technical support kits from regionally focused cryptologic shore support activities.

b. United States Army Intelligence and Security Command

United States Army Intelligence and Security Command (INSCOM) is the Army's SCE. It provides support to deployed MAGTFs when—

- Marines are part of a joint force that includes Army SIGINT units.
- Marines are serving as part of a larger force that includes adjacent Army units.
- Army theater fixed-site activity or mobile SIGINT asset can provide support.

c. Air Intelligence Agency

Air Force Intelligence Agency (AIA) is the Ai Force's SCE. Its elements support deployed MAGTFs by collecting and producing air intelligence or by providing SIGINT support for air and air defense operations.

2003. National SIGINT Organizations

a. National Security Agency

In order to provide timely, effective SIGINT support to military commanders, NSA established several tailored support mechanisms.

(1) National Security Operations Center.

The NSOC supports JTF and MAGTF operations by providing SIGINT reporting derived from national assets. The NSOC functions as the current operations and crisis management center of the NSA to ensure that time-sensitive SIGINT needs of commanders are satisfied. The NSOC works closely with the National Military Command Center (NMCC) and other Department of Defense (DOD) I&W watch centers.

(2) Regional Security Operations Centers.

NSA established three RSOCs to enhance SIGINT support to combatant commanders at all echelons. RSOCs are regionally focused and receive inputs from multiple sources. The RSOCs are located at Fort Gordon, Georgia; San Antonio, Texas; and Kunia, Hawaii.

The following organizations are established at each RSOC:

- NSG established a cryptologic shore support activity (CSSA) staffed with Marine and Navy personnel at each RSOC. CSSAs provide direct support to naval tactical operations through interface with the RSOC. This interface allows greater tailoring of RSOC operations supporting the intelligence requirements of MAGTF operations. Principal communications connectivity to CSSAs i provided by Navy communications systems within SSES.
- INSCOM established a technical control and analysis element (TCAE) at each of the RSOC locations. CSSA Marine personne interface with TCAE personnel to provide ground-oriented intelligence information in support of the MAGTF. Communication connectivity with the TCAEs is provided generally via the Trojan Spirit II communications system organic to the RadBns or communications battalions.

b. National Reconnaissance Office

The National Reconnaissance Office (NRO) provides critical support to United States SIGINT operations. NRO's mission is to enable United States global information superiority during peace and war. NRO is responsible for unique and innovative technology, large-scale systems engineering, development and acquisition, and operation of space reconnaissance systems and related intelligence activities to support global information superiority. NRO's capabilities include supporting I&W, monitoring arms control agreements and supporting military operations. The NRO ac-complishes its mission through ongoing research and development, acquisition, and operation o spaceborne and airborne intelligence data collection systems. NRO assets and capabilities may be requested to support MAGTF operations unde procedures described in the *Joint Tactical Exploitation of National Systems (J-TENS) Manual.*

Chapter 3

SIGINT Responsibilities in the MAGTF

The MAGTF commander is ultimately responsible for the conduct of MAGTF SIGINT operations. The MAGTF commander's staff, major subordinate commands (MSCs), specialized units, and theater or national level organizations assist the commander in execution of SIGINT responsibilities. This chapter focuses on the roles and responsibilities of Marine operating forces' staffs, MSCs, and specialized units.

3001. Commanders, Marine Corps Forces

Commanders, Marine Corps forces (COMMARFORs), are responsible for using their organic SIGINT assets effectively and for ensuring responsive national and theater support to subordinate commands. COMMARFORs—

- Review and validate SIGINT support requests from subordinate commands and ensure they receive the tailored support they require.
- Review and comment on cryptologic support plans (CSPs) prepared by NSA and theater combatant commanders for MAGTF operation plans (OPLANs).
- Coordinate SIGINT issues and requirements with the theater and national agencies in support of Marine Corps forces (MARFOR).
- Coordinate with theater and national SIGINT and all-source intelligence agencies and organizations to support MARFORs.
- Review, exercise, and if necessary, develop, interoperable CIS architectures to support the SIGINT effort.
- Coordinate between MARFOR and their subordinate commands to improve SIGINT interoperability, standardization, preparedness, and performance.

3002. MAGTF Staff Sections

a. G-2/S-2

All MAGTF intelligence and counterintelligence activities, to include SIGINT, are under the staff cognizance of the unit G-2/S-2. Within the bounds of the commander's SOTA, the G-2/S-2 is responsible for planning, directing, managing, and supervising the tasking and operations of SIGINT units organic to and supporting the MAGTF. The G-2/S-2—

- Develops and satisfies outstanding PIRs and IRs by planning, directing, integrating, and supervising organic SIGINT operations and other MAGTF all-source intelligence operations.
- Prepares MAGTF SIGINT plans and orders.
- Coordinates SIGINT collection (to include SIGINT amplifications and SIGINT time sensitive requirements), production, and dissemination requirements that are beyond the capability of the MAGTF and submits them to higher headquarters for JTF, theater, o national SIGINT support.
- Ensures routine and time-sensitive SIGINT information is rapidly processed, analyzed, and incorporated in all-source intelligence products, and rapidly disseminates this information to MAGTF and external units.
- Evaluates JTF, theater, and national SIGINT support to the MAGTF and adjusts stated requirements if necessary.
- Identifies, validates, and assists with resolution of SIGINT personnel and equipment resources deficiencies (e.g., insufficient linguists and special signal analysts expertise).
- Incorporates SIGINT in training exercises to improve MAGTF individual, collective, and unit readiness.

b. G-1/S-1

The manpower or personnel staff officer (G-1/S-1) is responsible for all SIGINT personnel requirements. Often it is necessary to augment organic SIGINT units with specially-trained personnel from outside the command. The G-1 S-1 either internally sources or forwards personnel augmentation requests developed by the G-2/S-2 to higher headquarters for action.

c. G-3/S-3

The G-3/S-3 is responsible for planning, coordinating, and supervising the tactical employmen of units. The G-3/S-3 coordinates the movement and operations of SIGINT units with the G-2/S-2 for integration in current and future operations planning. Because SIGINT units also provide certain EW capabilities, the G-3/S-3, normally via the electronic warfare officer (EWO), coordinates SIGINT units' tactical positioning to provide tactical EW and command and control warfare (C2W) support. Normally, as the principal staf SIGINT user, the G-3/S-3 has the primary responsibility for planning maneuver operations and fire support, which requires close coordination throughout the planning process to ensure effective SIGINT support.

d. G-4/S-4

The logistics staff officer (G-4/S-4) is responsible for the combat service support (CSS) of MAGTF SIGINT units. To ensure the required support i available, the G-4/S-4 develops CSS arrangements to meet the needs of the deployed SIGINT units (particularly SIGINT units' unique equipment logistics requirements).

e. G-6/S-6

The G-6/S-6 is responsible for providing and protecting internal and external MAGTF CIS connectivity and operations. The G-6/S-6—

- Coordinates or provides communication paths, network accesses, and frequencies for SIGINT organizations attached to and/or supporting the command.
- Provides representation for CIS matters within the EWCC, when it is established.

- Assists the unit security manager and G-3/S-3 in promoting personnel awareness o enemy SIGINT threat capabilities, signals security training, and unit signals security preparedness.

3003. MAGTF Intelligence Section Elements

The MAGTF intelligence section, resident in the MAGTF CE, is the focal point for MAGTF SIGINT planning and direction and is supported by the combat intelligence center (CIC). Depending on the size of the MAGTF, operational requirements or other factors, the CIC may consist of a number of subordinate elements.

a. Combat Intelligence Center

The CIC is established within the MAGTF CE. Performing the primary functions of the MAGTF intelligence section, the CIC includes the following subelements.

(1) All-Source Fusion Center The AFC is the primary MAGTF analysis and production element. It processes and produces all-source intelligence products in response to MAGTF requirements.

(2) Surveillance and Reconnaissance Center. The surveillance and reconnaissance cente (SARC) is the primary element for the supervision of MAGTF collection operations. It directs, coordinates, and monitors intelligence collections operations conducted by organic, attached, and direct support collection assets.

(3) Operations Control and Analysis Center. The OCAC is the main node for the command and control of RadBn SIGINT operation and the overall coordination of MAGTF SIGINT operations. It processes, analyzes, produces, and disseminates SIGINT-derived information and directs the ground-based EW activities of the RadBn.

b. Intelligence Section and SIGINT Unit Commanders and Officers in Charge

(1) Intelligence Operations Officer. The intelligence operations officer is responsible to the G-2/S-2 for the overall planning and execution of MAGTF all-source intelligence operations. The intelligence operations officer—

- Plans and implements a concept of intelligence operations based upon the mission threat, commander's intent, and concept of operations.

- Develops, consolidates, validates, and prioritizes recommended PIRs and IRs to support MAGTF planning and operations.

- Plans, develops, and directs MAGTF intelligence collections, production, and dissemination plans, to include the effective employment and integration of MAGTF multidiscipline intelligence and reconnaissance operations.

- Coordinates and integrates MAGTF intelligence operations with other components, JTF, theater, and national intelligence operations.

- Evaluates and improves MAGTF intelligence operations.

(2) SIGINT Officer. The SIO is responsible to the MAGTF G-2/S-2 for the planning, direction, and execution of MAGTF SIGINT operations. The SIO—

- Coordinates with other intelligence section staff officers, the RadBn CO or OIC, and the ACE G-2/S-2 (for VMAQ TERPES operations) to prepare SIGINT plans and order for the MAGTF.

- Coordinates with the collection management officer and RadBn and VMAQ TERPES planners to coordinate, plan, supervise, and assist SIGINT collection requirement and taskings for MAGTF operations.

- Coordinates with the SARC OIC, RadBn CO or OIC, VMAQ TERPES OIC, and G-3/ S-3 to coordinate the movement, operation, and reporting of SIGINT units.

- Coordinates with MAGTF AFC OIC, RadBn CO or OIC, and VMAQ TERPES OIC to coordinate MAGTF AFC analyst exchanges with RadBn TERPES COMINT and ELINT analysts and to coordinate the integration of SIGINT with all-source intelligence production.

- Coordinates with the dissemination officer to plan for the timely reporting of SIGINT-derived intelligence to MAGTF and external elements and the rapid handling of perishable SIGINT information.

- Coordinates with the G-6/S-6, Marine division (MARDIV) OICs, Marine aircraft wing (MAW) special security communications teams (SSCTs), and SIGINT unit OICs to plan and coordinate special intelligence communications paths and operations.

- Assists the intelligence operations officer with preparing and presenting special intelligence briefings and reports as required.

(3) Special Security Officer. The SSO is responsible to the commander for ensuring the command's adherence to SCI regulations and policies, security clearance procedures, and SCI materia handling. Generally, the SSO is the unit's senior intelligence officer. The SSO—

- Establishes and/or maintains a SCIF or TSCIFs to support SIGINT and other compartmented operations.

- Ensures that the command and all subordinate organizations have sufficient SCI billets to meet all potential operational requirements, to include the administration and management of unit SCI billets and SCI security investigations.

- Provides oversight, training, and supporting procedures for the conduct of SCI sanitization and dissemination within the MAGTF. This includes the determination of applicable authority for sanitization and authorized recipients of the sanitized material.

(4) Collections Management Officer. The collections management officer (CMO) is responsible for formulating detailed ICRs and tasking and coordinating internal and external collection operations to satisfy the requirements. The CMO receives PIRs and IRs from the intelligence operations officer and develops an integrated collection plan using organic and supporting resources.

In coordination with the SIO and SIGINT unit COs or OICs, the CMO—

- Determines and coordinates ICRs that may be tasked to organic or supporting SIGINT elements.
- Identifies ICRs and prepares requests for intelligence that are beyond organic capabilities and that must be submitted to higher headquarters and external agencies for satisfaction.

(5) MAGTF All-Source Fusion Center Officer in Charge. The MAGTF AFC OIC is primarily responsibile for managing and supervising the MAGTF's all-source intelligence production and processing effort. The MAGTF AFC OIC—

- Determines and coordinates MAGTF IPRs, to include SIGINT element products as well as all-source intelligence products.
- Maintains all-source automated intelligence data bases, files, workbooks, country studies, planning imagery, mapping and topographic resources, and other references.
- Administers, operates, and maintains intelligence processing and production systems both general service (GENSER) and SCI, e.g., joint deployable intelligence support system (JDISS) and intelligence analysis system (IAS).
- Analyzes and fuses all-source intelligence into tailored products in response to stated or anticipated PIRs and IRs, to include sanitized SCI products.
- Develops and maintains current and future intelligence situational, threat and environmental assessments, and target intelligence

based upon all-source analysis, interpretation, and integration.

(6) Surveillance and Reconnaissance Center Officer in Charge. The SARC OIC is responsible for coordinating and supervising the execution of the integrated organic, attached and direct support intelligence collection, and reconnaissance operations. The SARC OIC—

- Maintains the status of the following ongoing intelligence collection operations, to include deployed RadBn collection and direction finding teams:
  - Mission of all teams.
  - Locations and times of all restricted fire areas and reconnaissance areas of operations.
  - Time and method of radio reconnaissance team (RRT) insertion and extraction.
  - Primary and alternate communications plans.
  - Time of last contact.
  - Time of next contact.
- Coordinates and monitors the insertion and extraction of SIGINT and other intelligence elements.
- Coordinates RadBn and VMAQ TERPES elements' collection and reporting activities under the overall intelligence operations plan. Ensures SIGINT elements understand the collection plan and are able to carry out their responsibilities under the plan.
- Ensures other MAGTF C2 nodes (e.g., the current operations center, the fire support coordination center) are apprised of ongoing intelligence and reconnaissance operations.
- Receives routine and time-sensitive intelligence reports from deployed SIGINT collection teams; cross-cues or exchanges intelligence reports with other intelligence collectors, as appropriate; and rapidly disseminates intelligence to MAGTF C2 nodes and others in accordance with intelligence reporting criteria and dissemination plans.

(7) Dissemination Officer. The dissemination officer is responsible for the effective conduct of intelligence dissemination within the MAGTF. The dissemination officer—

- Determines and coordinates MAGTF IDRs, to include all-source IDRs as well as intelligence discipline-unique requirements.
- Recommends dissemination priorities.
- Advises on and selects dissemination means.
- Develops intelligence dissemination plans and coordinates with the G-6/S-6 supporting CIS architectures for both voice and data networked communications. Coordinates and integrates these plans and architectures with theater, joint force, and MAGTF CIS and intelligence plans and architectures.
- Monitors the flow and ensures timely delivery of intelligence throughout the MAGTF.

(8) SIGINT Unit Commanding Officer or Officer in Charge. The SIGINT unit CO or OIC is responsible for the effective conduct o SIGINT operations in support of the commander's intent and the operational and intelligence concept of operations. The SIGINT unit CO or OIC—

- Plans and employs SIGINT resources in response to the commander's intent, threat situation, MAGTF G-2/S-2's guidance a direction, and intelligence operations plan.
- Effects technical direction and control of MAGTF organic SIGINT collection, processing and exploitation, production, and dissemination operations. Also helps coordinate MAGTF SIGINT operations with JTF, theater, national, and other Service SIGINT agencies.
- Coordinates movement and operations of SIGINT units with MAGTF staff element and subordinate units' commanders. Ensures that all element movements are coordinated with the COC, fire support coordination center (FSCC), and SARC.

- Advises the G-2/S-2, SIO, intelligence operations officer, MAGTF AFC OIC, CMO, and dissemination officer on SIGINT employment and its integration with JTF, theater, and national SIGINT operations.

3004. Marine Divisions and Aircraft Wings

SIGINT activities of the MARDIVs and MAWs come under the staff cognizance of the respective G-2s. This includes the integration of SIGINT operations and products in support of unit operations and the operations of their organic SSCT. SSCTs provide special intelligence (SI) communications support to their commanders and designated subordinate elements.

3005. Radio Battalions

The 1st and 2d RadBns are the Marine Corps' principal organic, tactical, SIGINT direct support elements. The primary mission of the RadBn and its detachments is to provide tactical SIGINT support to MAGTFs. RadBns are discussed further in chapter 4.

3006. VMAQs

VMAQs of Marine aircraft group (MAG)-14 perform airborne electronic reconnaissance and, through the use of TERPES, produce ELINT reports and electronic order of battle (EOB) intelligence. Due to the unique capabilities of TERPES, the ACE will often be tasked with producing and maintaining the EOB to be used by all MAGT elements. VMAQs are discussed in chapter 5.

CHAPTER 4

Radio Battalion

The mission of radio battalions is to provide communications security (COMSEC) monitoring, tactical SIGINT, EW, and SI communication support to the MAGTF.

4001. Tasks

The radio battalion—

- Conducts interception, radio direction finding (DF), recording, and analysis of communications and noncommunications signals and SIGINT processing, analysis, production, and reporting.
- Conducts EW against enemy or other hostile communications.
- Assists in the protection of MAGTF communications from enemy exploitation by conducting COMSEC monitoring, analysis, and reporting on friendly force communications.
- Provides SI communications support and cryptographic guard (personnel and terminal equipment) in support of MAGTF command elements and RadBn operations. (Normally, communications connectivity for SI communications is provided by the communications unit supporting the MAGTF CE.)
- Provides task-organized detachments to MAGTFs with designated SIGINT, EW, SI communications, and other required capabilities.
- Exercises technical control and direction over MAGTF RadBn SIGINT and EW operations.
- Provides RRT with specialized insertion and extraction capabilities (e.g., combat rubber raiding craft, fast rope, rappel, helocast, static line parachute) to provide specified SIGINT and EA support during advance force, preassault, or deep postassault operations.

- Coordinates technical SIGINT requirements and exchanges SIGINT technical information and material with national, theater, joint, and other SIGINT units.
- Provides intermediate, third- and fourth-echelon maintenance of RadBn SIGINT and EW equipment.

4002. Organization

The 1st RadBn, Marine Corps Base (MCB), Kaneohe Bay, Hawaii, is subordinate to Commander, Marine Corps Forces, Pacific (COMMARFORPAC), and supports both I and III MEFs. The 2d RadBn, Camp Lejeune, North Carolina, is subordinate to II MEF. Both battalions are organized and equipped along functional lines to provide administrative control of subordinate elements, to facilitate training, and to permit rapid structuring and operational deployment o task-organized units or detachments.

The 1st RadBn is organized into a headquarter and service (H&S) company and three line companies (A, B, and C). The 2d RadBn is comprised of an H&S company and two line companies (A and B). See figure 4-1 on page 4-2. RadBns' line companies are not tactical organizations, but instead they serve as training and administrative units providing the basic unit structure around which task-organized SIGINT support units o detachments are trained, equipped, and formed Even if the entire RadBn were to deploy, it would task-organize for the mission assigned.

a. Headquarters and Service Company

The H&S company provides personnel and facilities with which the RadBn commander commands and controls battalion operations. It also provides service support for other battalion

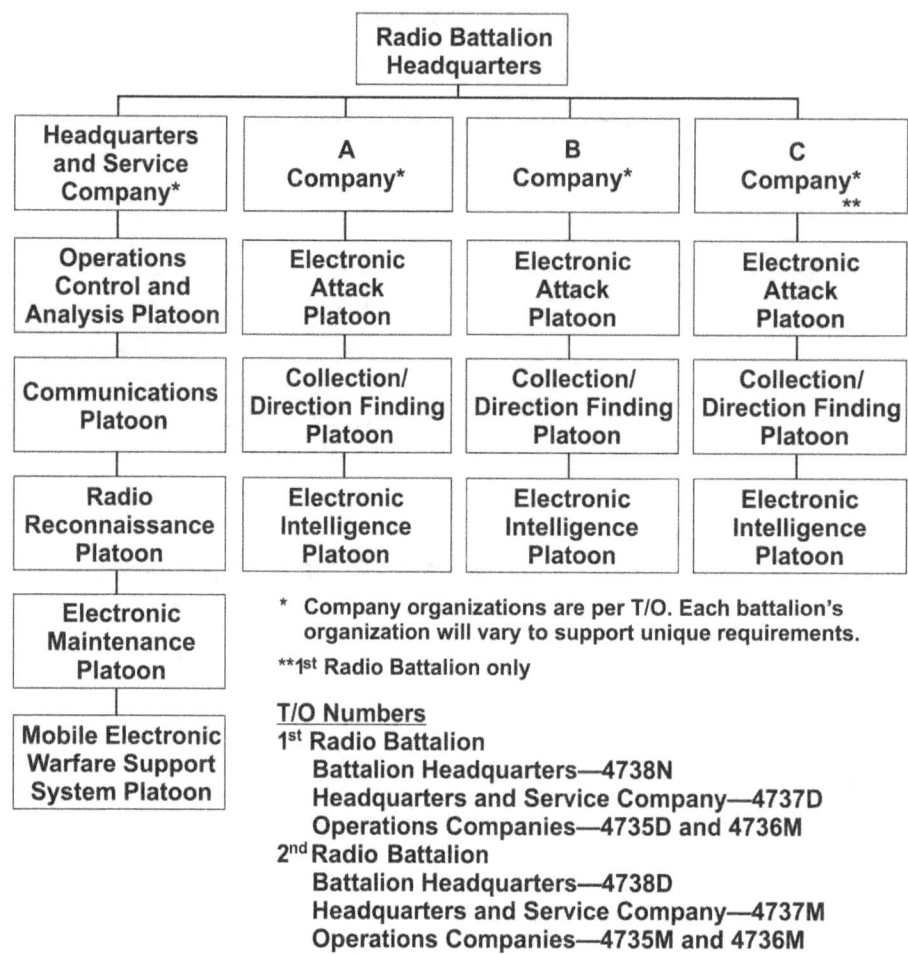

Figure 4-1. Radio Battalion Organization.

elements. Those tasks are accomplished by H&S staff sections (i.e., S-1, S-2, S-3, S-4, and S-6) and the following specialized platoons.

(1) Operations Control and Analysis Platoon. The operations control and analysis (OCA) platoon provides the Marines and equipment to perform RadBn operational planning and direction and SIGINT production, analysis, and reporting operations. Additionally, it is the nucleus for the RadBn OCAC during tactical operations.

(2) Communications Platoon. The communications platoon provides Marines and equipment to conduct special security communications operations in support of RadBn and, when deployed, MAGTF CE operations. Additionally, the platoon is equipped to support RadBn's internal communications requirements.

(3) Radio Reconnaissance Platoon. The radio reconnaissance platoon (RRP) provides trained RRTs for operations during advance force, preassault, or other operations where the employment of conventional RadBn teams may be inappropriate or unfeasible.

(4) Electronic Maintenance Platoon. The electronic maintenance platoon provides up to fourth-echelon maintenance support on RadBn unique equipment and second-echelon support on Marine Corps common communications and electronics equipment.

(5) Mobile Electronic Warfare Support System Platoon. Using a light armored vehicle (LAV) variant platform, the mobile electronic warfare support system (MEWSS) platoon provides Marines and equipment capable of SIGINT

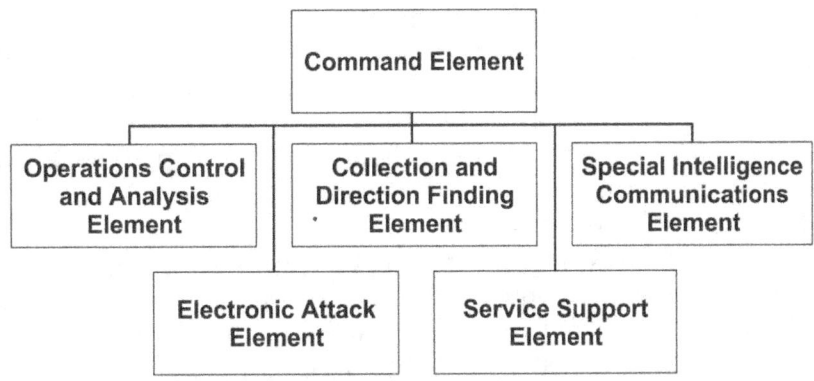

Figure 4-2. SIGINT Support Unit Elements.

collection, DF, reporting, and communication jamming operations.

b. Operational Companies

Each RadBn operational company has a table of organization (T/O) of 5 officers and 100 enlisted Marines organized into a company headquarters, EA platoon, voice collection and DF platoon, and nonvoice or ELINT collection platoon. During tactical operations, the company will be task-organized or reinforced with battalion assets consistent with the threat, mission, commander's intent, and intelligence concept of operations.

4003. Task Organization for MAGTF Operations SIGINT Support Unit

An entire RadBn will support a MEF operation To support smaller MAGTFs, the RadBn's tactical organization is the task-organized SIGINT support unit (SSU). The SSU may be as large as an operational company (minus or reinforced) or as small as a four-Marine team. The RadBn organization enables the rapid structuring and operational deployment of task-organized SSUs.

a. SIGINT Support Unit Structure

A fully structured SSU containing all the capabilities found in the RadBn is comprised of six basic elements (see figure 4-2). The nature of the threat, specific mission tasking, and intelligence and op-

erational requirements determine the composition and equipment of each element.

(1) Command Element. The RadBn CO w designate an OIC and/or a staff noncommissioned officer in charge (SNCOIC) for each SSU. The command element is comprised of the personnel and facilities to command and control the SSU For smaller SSUs, the command element may be integrated within the operations control and analysis element with an OIC or an operations officer, noncommissioned officer in charge or an operations chief, and sufficient resources for command and control of the SSU operations. When the majority of the battalion deploys, the command element consists of the battalion commander, executive officer, sergeant major, and sufficien personnel for command and administrative support.

(2) Operations Control and Analysis Element. The SSU's command and control, analysis, production, and dissemination functions are executed within the OCAC. The OCAC performs the SIGINT processing, analysis, exploitation, production, and reporting of signals intelligence products and information. Additionally, it is the principle element that coordinates with other intelligence nodes to plan, direct, and integrate SIGINT operations with other intelligence and reconnaissance operations. Marines assigned to this element include the operations watch officers or operations watch chiefs, COMINT and ELIN analysts, translators or transcribers, and SIGINT report writers.

(3) Collection and Direction Finding Element. The collection and DF element is comprised of SIGINT support teams (SSTs) and other collection elements consisting of Marines and equipment for conducting SSU SIGINT collection and DF operations. Personnel assigned to this element include SIGINT linguists (or voice intercept operators), manual-Morse, non-Morse, and ELINT collection and DF operators, and supervisory personnel. Additionally, this element may contain MEWSS- or RRT-capable SSTs if the mission or situation warrants.

(4) Electronic Attack Element. The EA element is comprised of the Marines and equipment to conduct EA operations. Personnel assigned to this element include EA supervisors or controllers and EA operators.

(5) Special Intelligence Communications Element. The SI communications element installs and operates the SI or special security communications terminals for the SSU and the MAGTF CE. In addition, the SI communications element will install and operate SCI-level LAN systems to support SSU operations. The systems installed will depend on the mission, intelligence and CIS operations concepts, connectivity requirements, and terminal equipment availability. Personnel assigned to this element include communications supervisory personnel, information systems security and system administrators, and communications operators.

(6) Service Support Element. The service support element provides limited supply, engineers, electronic maintenance, and medical support to the SSU. The SSU depends on the MAGTF combat service support element (CSSE) for most of its combat service support. Marine assigned to the service support element may include medical, electronic maintenance, motor transport, engineer, supply, and administrative personnel.

b. SIGINT Support Unit Task-Organizational Considerations

SSUs are task-organized from resources available throughout the RadBn and are tailored to the requirements of the supported commander. The SSU's specific size and composition will also be influenced by threat and environmental factors known or expected to be encountered in the intended area of operations. The following factors must be considered when task-organizing an SSU.

(1) Enemy Signals Environment. The prime factor in determining the size, composition, and capabilities of an SSU is the known or anticipated enemy signals environment. Enemy factors to consider are—

- Target power output and frequency range.
- Digital or analog signals.
- Modulation techniques.
- Target signal operating instructions (i.e., sophisticated or complex).
- Target emitters (i.e., number, type, and density).

(2) Physical Environment. Terrain, climate, vegetation, and the operations area size influence the size and composition of the SSU.

(3) Operational Environment. Among factors that must be considered are—

- The military and political situation.
- The adversary's—
  - Size.
  - Composition.
  - Disposition.
  - C2 and CIS operations.
  - Doctrine, tactics, techniques, and procedures.
- The friendly force's—
  - Composition.
  - Commander's intent.
  - Operational and intelligence concepts.
  - Task organization.
  - Mobility.

c. SIGINT Support Unit Operations Watch Structure

The SSU must be capable of sustained, 24-hou operations. SSU elements, excepting the service support element, are normally employed in two or three watch sections. In large SSUs, each watch section may have an officer and/or a staff non-commissioned officer (SNCO) assigned as an operations watch officer (OWO) or operations watch chief (OWC). In smaller SSUs, this function may be performed by a noncommissioned officer (NCO).

4004. Command and Control

a. Command Relationships

(1) Operational Control. The MAGTF commander with SOTA has OPCON of RadBn, which is exercised by the MAGTF G-2/S-2 and executed by the RadBn OIC.

(2) Administrative Control. Administrative control (ADCON) of RadBn SSUs is exercised by the unit to which the SSU is attached (in most cases the MAGTF CE).

(3) SIGINT Technical Control. SIGINT technical control (TECHCON) of United States SIGINT system assets, to include RadBn SSUs, is always retained by DIRNSA who delegates SOTA to MAGTF commanders. This means that within the MAGTF, the MAGTF commander with SOTA generally retains, coordinates, and exercises SIGINT TECHCON regardless of any other C2 relationships established for the operation (e.g., RadBn elements attached to or placed in direct support of MAGTF subordinate elements).

b. Support Relationships

The MAGTF commander may establish variou support relationships between the SSU and MAGTF subordinate elements when one organization should aid, protect, complement, or sustain another unit. The nature of the support relationship will be specified by a directive (e.g., annex B of the operations order) which should detail—

- Forces and other resources allocated to the subordinate element of the SSU.

- Time, place, level, and duration of the SSU support effort.
- Priority of the SSU supporting effort.
- Command relationships and degree of authority granted to the supported commander.

The two most common support relationships fo SSUs are general and direct support.

(1) General Support General support (GS) is action given to the MAGTF as a whole rather than to a particular subordinate element. Given the nature of SIGINT operations, GS is the most common support relationship used for SSU operations.

(2) Direct Support. Direct support (DS) is a mission requiring a force to support another specific force and authorizing it to answer directly the supported force's requests for assistance. When required by the mission and situation, elements of a SSU may be placed in DS of MAGTF subordinate elements (e.g., elements of the SSU in DS of the GCE).

4005. Notional Concepts of Employment and Task Organizations

The mission, enemy or other potentially hostile elements, and operational environment will always influence the composition and employment of SIGINT assets, as will logistics concerns such as footprint or airlift availability. To serve as a planning departure point, RadBns have developed notional SSU packages and concepts of employment which will be refined as mission and adversary details become known. (Appendix A, Radio Battalion SIGINT Support Unit Checklist, is provided as an SSU operations planning guide.) The levels of RadBn support can range from electronic collocation with the supported unit to an entire RadBn (minus or reinforced) deploying with a MEF as indicated by the following examples. It is important to note that no specific RadBn SSU may ever match exactly the following notional descriptions due to task organization, personnel or equipment availability, and mission and threat considerations.

a. Marine Expeditionary Unit (Special Operations Capable) SIGINT Support Unit

The SSU concept of employment is dependent on the Marine expeditionary unit's (MEU) mission, threat, and planned concept of operations. The SSU is attached to the CE and almost always is employed in general support of the MEU (special operations capable [SOC]).

Generally, MEU(SOC) SSUs consist of 1 officer as the OIC, possibly another officer as the assistant OIC, and 20 or more enlisted Marines (to normally include at least one RRT). Table 4-1 provides a notional MEU(SOC) SSU T/O.

b. Fly-In Echelon

The fly-in echelon (FIE) is integrated and task organized to provide immediate SIGINT, EW, and SI communications in support of lead elements of a MAGTF or to reinforce MEU(SOC SSU capabilities. The FIE serves as the foundation for the buildup of SIGINT assets as required. Figure 4-3 illustrates a notional FIE configuration. The FIE generally consists of 2 officers and 18 to 30 enlisted Marines. Table 4-2 provides a typical FIE T/O. The FIE is under the operational control of the MAGTF commander who exercises SOTA. Initial operations will be in general support of MAGTF requirements. As the situation matures and the mission and associated tasks become clearer, the task organization and command relationships of the FIE or SSU elements may be modified to provide direct support to designated major subordinate elements (MSEs).

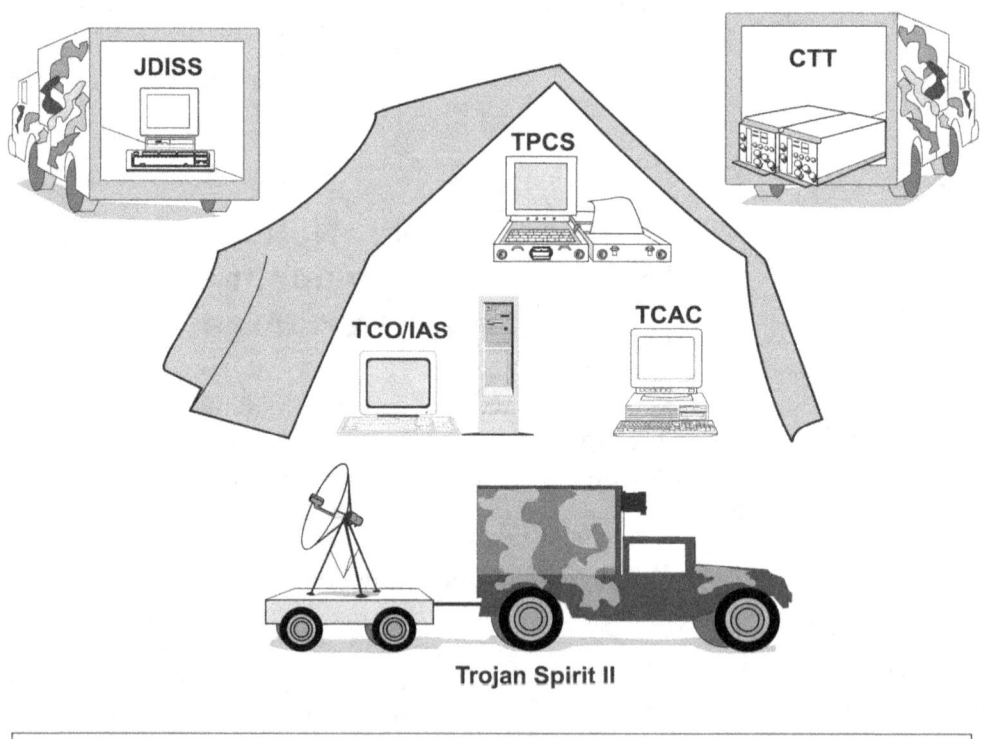

Trojan Spirit II

Legend	
CTT=Commander's Tactical Terminal	TCO=Tactical Combat Operations
TCAC=Technical Control and Analysis Center	TPCS=Team Portable Collection System

Figure 4-3. Notional SSU Fly-In Echelon Configuration.

Table 4-1. Notional MEU(SOC) SSU T/O.

Billet	Rank	MOS
H&S Support Elemen		
OIC	Capt	0202/0206
Assistant OIC	Lt	0206
SNCOIC	GySgt	2621/2629
Electronic maintenance technicia	Cpl	2841
SI CIS chief	Sgt	2651
LAV mechanic	LCpl-Sgt	2147
OCA Element		
Processing and reporting chief	SSgt	2621/2629
ELINT analyst	Sgt	2631
Signals analyst	Sgt	2621/2629
Collection/DF Team #1 (MEWSS capable)		
Team leader	SSgt	2621/2629
Linguist or voice intercept operator	Sgt	267X
Linguist or voice intercept operator	Cpl	267X
Manual morse or DF operator	LCpl	2621
EA operator	LCpl	2621
Collection/DF Team #2 (Helo capable)		
Team leader	Sgt	2621/2629
Linguist or voice intercept operator	Cpl	267X
Linguist or voice intercept operator	LCpl	267X
Collection or DF operator	LCpl	2621
Collection/DF Team #3 (RRT capable		
Team leader	SSgt	2621/2629
Assistant team leader	Sgt	267X
Linguist or voice intercept operator	Cpl	267X
Linguist or voice intercept operator	LCpl	267X
Collection or DF operator	Cpl	2621
Collection or DF operator	LCpl	2621

Table 4-2. Notional Fly-In Echelon T/O.

Billet	Rank	MOS
H&S Support Elemen		
OIC	Capt	0202/0206
SNCOIC	MSgt	2691
Electronic maintenance technicia	Sgt	2841
SI Communications Element		
Communications chief	SSgt	2651
Trojan Spirit operator[1]	Sgt	2651
Trojan Spirit operator	LCpl	2651
Communications operator	Cpl	2651
Communications operator	LCpl	2651
OCA Elemen		
Operations officer	Lt	0206
Senior analyst	GySgt	267X/2629
Analyst	SSgt	2621/2629
Analyst	Sgt	2621/2629
Signals chief	SSgt	2621/2629
Signals analyst	Sgt	2621
Signals analyst	Cpl	2621
ELINT analyst	Sgt	2631
ELINT analyst	LCpl	2631
Collection/DF Element		
Team leader	SSgt	2621/2629
Linguist or voice intercept operator	Sgt	267X
Linguist or voice intercept operator	Cpl	267X
Collection or DF operator	Cpl	2621

[1] 2nd RadBn does not have Trojan Spirit

c. Marine Expeditionary Force Support

For detailed SIGINT support information regarding a specific MEF operation, refer to the CSP and annex B of the OPLAN for that operation The following is a discussion of RadBn support of a notional MEF operation.

(1) **Concept of Operations** A MEF-level operation is supported by the RadBn (minus or reinforced. It could be minus because prior committed RadBn assets, such as MEU SSUs, were unavailable. It could be reinforced because some level of personnel or equipment augmentation from the other RadBn, MarSptBn, and/or Marine Corps units might be required.

(2) **Concept of Employment.** The RadBn task-organizes and employs its companies and teams to best support the MEF by—

- Deploying collection or DF teams for improved target signals access and operational support to forward MAGTF units.
- Collocating RadBn's C2 node with the MAGTF G-2/S-2's CIC and operating within the integrated intelligence concept of operations in GS of the MAGTF.
- Focusing on tasked PIRs and IRs and providing required support to all six intelligence functions.
- Disseminating time-sensitive SIGINT products to subordinate MAGTF units when required by the tactical situation.
- Providing OCAC liaison teams (OLTs) to the lead elements of the MEF, its MSEs and adjacent units as required; and providing SIGINT support elements (SSEs) and SSTs with mobile MAGTF units.
- Providing security and CIS for all internal RadBn requirements and for specified MAGTF CE support.
- Integrating operations with other MAGTF intelligence units to support cueing of other intelligence and reconnaissance collection elements, all-source intelligence production, and other mutual support.

(3) **Company Command Element.** One of the keys to effective MEF support is the placemen and use of the company command elements (CCEs). The CCEs are normally collocated with the GCE or MAGTF-subordinate task force headquarters depending on the mission and threat.

The CCE—

- Provides I&W support to the supported commanders.
- Coordinates location, operations, and support of SSTs with supported units and other forward-deployed intelligence and reconnaissance units.
- Serves as the C2, communications, and SIGINT-tasking channel between the OCAC and forward-deployed SST as required.
- Provides company liaison teams (CLTs) to adjacent and subordinate units as required.
- Provides or arranges for SST administration, logistic, and physical security support.
- Provides SIGINT tasking and direction of SSTs when the OCAC is unable to provide tasking and direction.

d. **Radio Reconnaissance Teams**

RRTs are six-Marine teams trained in special insert or extract means and basic amphibious reconnaissance capabilities. This additional training makes the RRT capable of advance force, preassault, deep postassault, and maritime special purpose force (MSPF) SIGINT missions as assigned. RRTs support the six intelligence functions. Additionally, they may be tasked to conduct SIGINT signals search and data base development in order to enhance understanding of threat operations prior to the arrival of other SSU forces. In an advance force role, RRTs may be employed to—

- Provide SIGINT-derived I&W intelligence support to advance forces.
- Provide SIGINT collection and reporting in areas not accessible to conventional SSTs.
- Provide SIGINT collection and reporting in support of assault and landing forces.
- Provide collection of unique signals. Unique signals are signals expected to have intelligence value that cannot be collected by other reasonable means (e.g., low-powered UHF communications).
- Conduct threat signals search and data base development.

e. Mobile Electronic Warfare Support System SIGINT Support Team

The principal advantage of a MEWSS SST is its high mobility, light armored protection, allowing it to maintain operations and provide direct support of similarly equipped ground combat element units. The employment of MEWSS vehicles requires close coordination with both the G-2/S-2 and G-3/S-3 as the MEWSS provides the only ground-based ELINT collection and the major ground-based communications EA capabilities organic to the MAGTF. The COMINT capabilities of the MEWSS are similar to that of any SST.

f. Aviation SIGINT Support Team

The aviation SSTs capabilities are similar to those of other SSTs. Its principal advantage is the ability to operate aboard Marine aviation platforms (e.g., helicopters). Aviation SSTs can provide SIGINT support to air and airborne units during missions such as deep raids and tactical recovery of aircraft and personnel operations or when the MAGTF commander needs immediate I&W accessible only by airborne SIGINT collection elements. The use of airborne SIGINT operation provides supporting SSTs with the ability to collect and exploit threat signals from extended ranges. The basic aviation SST is task-organized consistent with the mission and supported force's requirements. Generally, an aviation SST consists of RadBn Marines with a COMINT receiver, intelligence broadcast receiver, communications jammer, and UHF satellite communications radio.

g. Operations Control and Analysis Center Liaison Team

An OLT supports the intelligence effort of MAGTF subordinate elements (e.g., ACE or CSSE headquarters or rear area operations center). OLTs collocate with the G-2/S-2 of the supported unit operating from within its TSCIF. The OLT is task-organized out of available SSU assets in tactical support of the organization to which it is assigned. This assignment could be for a specific operation, phase, or for the duration of a conflict. Primarily, OLTs provide additional SIGINT

C2 support and CIS connectivity for tactical SIGINT planning, production, and reporting with the MAGTF G-2/S-2 and RadBn OCAC. OLTs expedite, simplify, and coordinate the sharing of SIGINT I&W, technical data, taskings, and products. Normally, the OLT monitors RadBn collection teams and theater SIGINT reporting communications to provide the supported unit access to tactical and operational-level SIGINT and I&W intelligence. In most cases, an OLT will consists of at least one officer and three enlisted Marines with supporting CIS equipment.

h. Company Liaison Team

A CLT is task-organized with available assets to best satisfy the requirements of the organization or unit to which it is assigned (e.g., an infantry battalion). This assignment is normally for a specific duration or operational phase. In most cases, a CLT will consist of one SNCO and one to three additional enlisted Marines. Like the OLT, the CLT expedites SIGINT I&W to local decisionmakers and assists with SST employment, tasking, and support.

i. Augmentation and Composition

Due to the low density of many SIGINT skills and equipment and the high tempo of operations, the RadBns may lack sufficient personnel with the requisite skills or SIGINT equipment with the necessary capabilities for a particular operation RadBns are reinforced with personnel and SIGINT equipment by augmenting and compositing.

For a small number of personnel requirements, individual augmentation often works best. With concurrence from the supported organization, the RadBn will forward a request for SIGINT personnel augmentation to CMC (C4I or CIS) via the COMMARFOR (G-1/G-2). Once the request is received at CMC, it will be validated and forwarded to CNSG and MarSptBn. MarSptBn will attempt to satisfy the request with active and/o reserve Marines from the battalion. Any portion of the request that MarSptBn can not satisfy will be returned to CMC (C4I/CIS) for sourcing from other Marine Corps units or other sources.

For significant numbers of personnel and equipment in support of a large operation or major regional contingency, elements may be composited from one RadBn with the other RadBn. Coordination between the RadBns should be continuous in the development of contingency plans (CONPLANs), OPLANs, and CSPs to ensure mutual understanding and validation of requirements and information (e.g., time-phased force deployment data).

Chapter 5

Marine Tactical Electronic Warfare Squadrons

Marine aviation performs six functions: offensive air support (OAS), antiair warfare (AAW), assault support, aerial reconnaissance, EW, and C2 of aircraft and missiles. VMAQs provide the MAGTF and other designated forces with EW support. The VMAQ also has an inherent capability to perform visual and electronic air reconnaissance. Electronic reconnaissance is the detection, identification, evaluation, and location of foreign electromagnetic radiation to provide EOB information. This chapter will focus on the VMAQ electronic reconnaissance and ELINT capabilities.

5001. Mission and Tasks

VMAQs provide EW (principally EA) and ELINT support to the MAGTF and other designated forces. When deployed, the VMAQ is under the operational and administrative control of the ACE commander. To support the MAGTF, the VMAQ conducts tactical jamming to prevent, delay, or interrupt detection and tracking by enemy early warning, acquisition, fire or missile control, counterbattery, and battlefield surveillance radars. Tactical jamming also denies and/or degrades enemy communications capabilities.

In addition, the VMAQ conducts electronic reconnaissance and ELINT operations to maintain EOB, to include both selected emitter parameters and location of nonfriendly emitters. VMAQs also provide threat warnings for friendly aircraft, ships, and ground units.

Key VMAQ tasks include—

- Providing aerial EA and ES support to ACE and other designated operations.
- Processing, analyzing, and producing routine and time-sensitive ELINT reports fo

updating and maintaining enemy EOB. This is accomplished through the intelligence and electronic warfare division, TERPES, and the tactical EA-6B mission planning system (TEAMS) sections to support premission planning and postmission processing of collected data and production of pertinent intelligence reports. Working in concert with the intelligence section, TERPES and TEAMS sections provide required ELINT and EOB intelligence products to the ACE and MAGTF.

- Providing liaison personnel to ACE and MAGTF CE staffs to assist in VMAQ employment planning. Inherent in this task i the requirement to provide an air EW liaison officer to the MAGTF EWCC.
- Conducting EA operations for EP training of MAGTF units.
- Intercepting, recording, and jamming threat communications and noncommunication emitters.

5002. Organization and Concept of Employment

There are four VMAQs (designated VMAQ-1 through VMAQ-4) assigned to MAG-14, 2d MAW, Cherry Point, North Carolina. Each squadron has five EA-6B Prowler aircraft and is organized into administrative, intelligence and electronic warfare, operations, logistics, safety and standardization, and maintenance divisions See figures 5-1 and 5-2 on page 5-2.

EA-6B aircraft conduct EA, ELINT, and electronic reconnaissance operations in support of ACE and other MAGTF missions. The TERPES section functions as a key element of the MAGTF's intelligence operations. TERPES is an

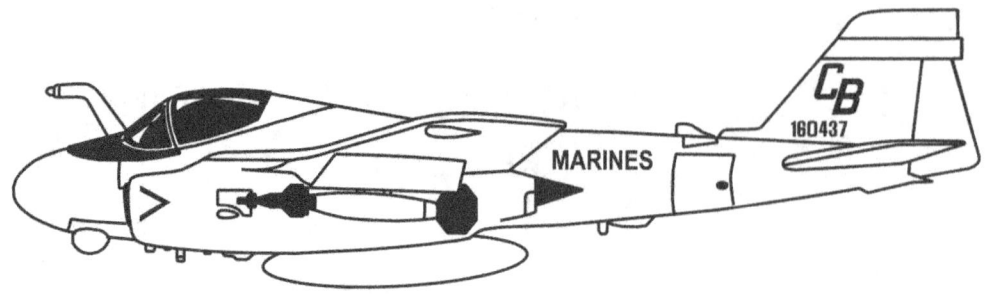

Figure 5-1. EA-6B Prowler

air-transportable, land-mobile intelligence processing and production system organic to VMAQ and is used to develop, maintain, and distribute tactical EOB and ELINT reports. TERPES functions as an automated tactical data system capable of producing current and future intelligence through information storage and retrieval, data recording, data base management, and data comparison. TERPES has a stand-alone capability but is utilized by VMAQs to optimize signals analysi and reporting to support MAGTF operations. Figure 5-3 provides an overview of VMAQ and TERPES operations.

5003. EA-6B Prowler

The EA-6B Prowler is a subsonic, all-weather, carrier-capable aircraft. The crew is composed of one pilot and three electronic countermeasure officers. The Prowler's primary missions include collecting and processing designated threat SO for jamming and subsequent processing, analysis, and intelligence reporting; and employing the AGM-88 high-speed antiradiation missile (HARM) against designated targets. The AN/ALQ-99 Tactical Jamming System effectively

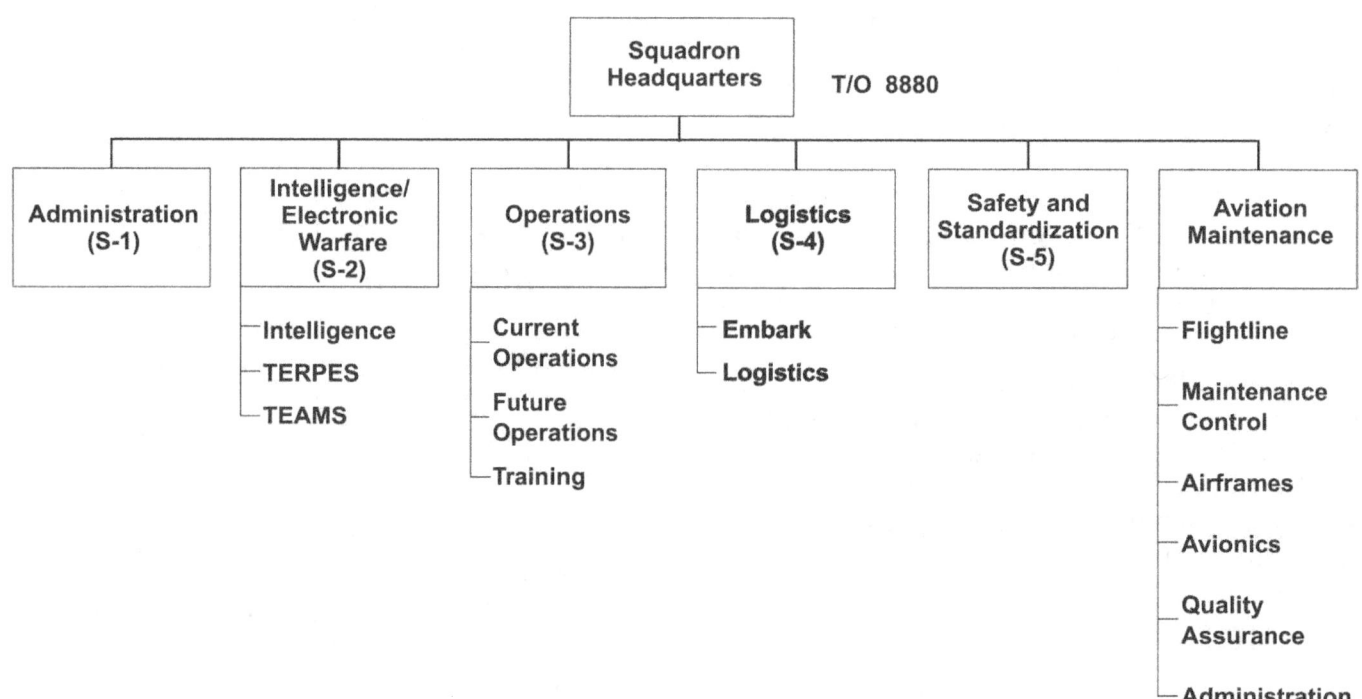

Figure 5-2. VMAQ Organization.

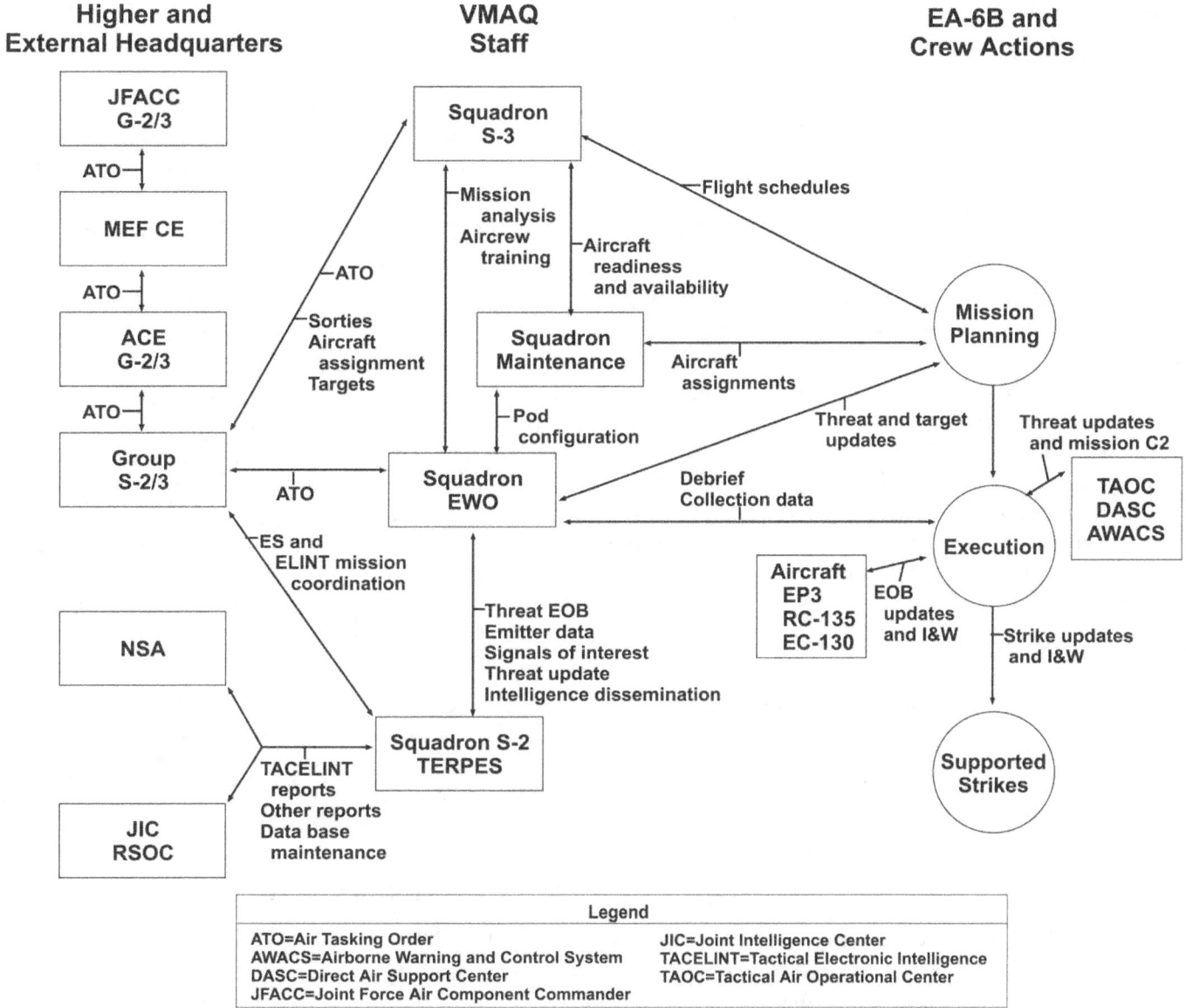

Figure 5-3. VMAQ and TERPES Operations.

incorporates receivers and external pods for signals reception and transmission of jamming signals (principally those associated with threat air defense radars and associated C2).

In addition to the AN/ALQ-99, the EA-6B also employs the USQ-113 Communications Suite which provides the ability to collect, record, and

disrupt threat communications in either of the following two modes of operation:

- EA which scans the electromagnetic environment to intercept and jam targeted signals of interest (SOIs).
- ES which scans the electromagnetic environment to intercept and digitally record SOIs.

5004. Tactical EA-6B Mission Planning System

TEAMS is designed to assist EA-6B aircrew with planning allocation and optimization of receivers, jammers, HARM, and other integrated weapon systems into a comprehensive C2W package. Basic intelligence data is provided by various MAGTF theater and other intelligence and analysis centers. Parametric data for friendly and adversary platforms, weapons systems, and emitters is provided by the electronic warfare data base system (EWDS) on a quarterly basis and near-real-time updates may be provided through tactical receive equipment (TRE) integrated by the TERPES section into the TEAMS workstation. World maps, terrain data, and digitized navigation charts are provided by the National Imagery and Mapping Agency (NIMA) on a quarterly basis.

TEAMS allows the operator to—

- Maintain area of operations emitter listings.
- Edit emitter parameters.
- Develop mission-specific geographic data and EOB.
- Perform postflight mission analysis to—
  - Identify electronic emitters using various electronic parameter data bases and ELINT analytical techniques.
  - Locate emitters by coordinates with a certain circular error of probability for each site.
  - Correlate new information with existing data.
- Accomplish mission planning in support of coordinated strikes and EA-6B optimization.

5005. TERPES

TERPES (AN/TSQ-90) is an air- and land-transportable, single-shelter ELINT processing and correlation system. The TERPES team is composed of Marines, equipment, software, and supporting procedures integrated to—

- Identify and locate enemy radar emitters from data collected by EA-6B aircraft o those received from other intelligence sources.
- Process and disseminate EW data rapidly to MAGTF intelligence centers.
- Provide mission planning and briefing support to VMAQ EA and ES operations.

The standard TERPES configuration consists o one 8- by 8- by 20-foot shelter and two skid-mounted environmental control units (ECUs). Positioned on and around the shelters are a TRE antenna, an HF antenna, and two mast-mounted UHF antennas. These modules can be tailored to specific mission requirements. Electrical powe support for TERPES must be obtained from the Marine wing support squadron.

The TERPES is operated by one MOS 2602 SIGINT/EW warrant officer and six MOS 2631 TERPES operators/analysts. Maintenance support i provided by one MOS 9966 TSQ-90 maintenance officer and four MOS 2821 TSQ-90 technicians.

a. Operational Capabilities

The TERPES will—

- Translate rapidly the machine-readable, airborne-collected digital data into man- and machine-readable reports (i.e., paper, magnetic tape, secure voice, plots, and overlays).
- Receive and process EA-6B mission tapes.
- Accept, correlate, and identify electronic emitters data from semiautomatic or automatic collection systems using various electronic parameter data bases and ELINT analytical techniques.
- Locate emitters by coordinates with a certain circular error of probability for each site.

- Provide EA-6B EWOs with tactical intelligence briefings to support EA and ES missions. (The official title for EWO is electronic countermeasures officer [ECMO]. EWO is used to accurately reflect the scope of MOS 7588 activities and EW terminology changes.)
- Provide tactical jamming analysis.
- Ensure tactical intelligence data base maintenance for the VMAQ and the EOB for the MAGTF.

b. Mapping Package

The TERPES mapping and overlay package is based on NIMA products which have been integrated into a software program called the Delorme mapping system. This system allows TERPES operators to display mapping data that is loaded to the TERPES system at scales ranging from worldwide scale down to the 1:5,000 scale. A wide range of tools such as zoom, projection magnification, perspective, linear, and spatial analysis allow operators to manipulate mapping data to enhance understanding of the overlaid threat information.

c. Intelligence Analysis

The TERPES Intelligence Analysis Application (IAA) enables the operator to analyze ELINT data combined with additional modernized integrated data base (MIDB) intelligence data to—

- Respond to requests for intelligence (RFIs).
- Prepare intelligence data base updates.
- Analyze threat and tactical situations.
- Estimate changes in the threat's tactical situation.

d. Data Fusion

MIDB is the primary intelligence data base for IAA operator queries. In addition to EA-6B aircraft mission tapes, other inputs required to maximize the support provided to tactical intelligence operations include the following:

- Naval intelligence data base (NID) contains characteristics and performance data for weapons, sensors, and platforms.
- EWDS is similar to the NID and provides EA-6B tailored data.
- ELINT parameters list (EPL) is NSA's observed radar parametric data.
- Electronic warfare integrated reprogramming (EWIR) is produced by the United States Air Force Foreign Technology Division. EWIR combines assessed technical radar parameters from the United States Air Force EW Science and Technology data base with the observed parameters of the NSA data base.
- Joint spectrum center (JSC) is used to derive friendly EOB and radar parametric data.

e. TERPES Fusion Processor

The TERPES fusion processor (TFP) processe intelligence data from tactical ELINT (TACELINT) reports, tactical reports (TACREPs), and IMINT reports. The TFP provides filtering, characteristic and performance identification, order of battle (OOB) identification, technical analysis, multisource correlation, and candidate updates. The TFP presents the information in various forms for analysis. One TFP integrated information source is the TRE and Related Applications (TRAP) broadcast. This broadcast is accessed using the TRE and provides near-real-time (NRT), national-level reports to the TERPES. The TRAP broadcast also assists the TFP in maintaining an ELINT parameter data base to track airborne, shipboard, and land-based targets as a tool to develop EOBs and as an instrument to perform comparative studies on radar parameters.

f. TERPES ELINT Preprocessor

The TERPES ELINT preprocessor (TEPP) processes all EA-6B SOI collected from recorder o reproducer set tape or disk files. Specifically, the application allows for the NRT analysis of technical ELINT data. Position reports and specific unit identification and location information are used to update the TERPES data base and to prepare TA-CELINT reports. TERPES also provides tactical jamming system (TJS) analysis for the EA-6B aircrew and maintenance personnel.

TJS analysis consists of recovering recorded data for verifying jammer calibration, on- and off-jammer times, and frequency and azimuth coverage. TERPES will use mission data in the generation of EW mission summary reports.

g. Intelligence Reporting

The primary intelligence output from TERPES operations is mission reports. Mission reports are available in many forms and are provided primarily to MAGTF intelligence elements in response to established intelligence requirements. The most commonly used reporting form is the TACELINT (refer to USSID 340, *Tactical ELINT Reporting*, for format and content).

Other report forms include the following:

- TACREP provides information on immediate threat activity.

- ELINT summary report provides a summary of ELINT activity over established periods (normally 24 hours). Refer to USSID 200 *Technical SIGINT Reporting*, for format and content.

- ELINT technical report provides for analyst exchange of information of parametric data. Refer to USSID 341, *Technical ELINT Reporting*, for format and content.

- Over the horizon (OTH) "GOLD" report provides information derived from contac reports of ELINT parametrics.

- Order of battle report (OBREP) provides order of battle information such as basic encyclopedia (BE) number, equipment, and location.

Chapter 6

Communications and Information Systems

The area of SIGINT operations currently undergoing substantial change is SIGINT CIS technological advances and architectures development. SIGINT architectures are changing from the use of separate, secure, 24-hour manned communications centers with dedicated, bulk-encrypted links to the use of multilevel information system security initiative (MISSI) capabilities over unsecured commercial or DOD networks via the Defens Message System (DMS). Adding the proliferation of SIGINT collection, processing, and production systems and centers along with other intelligence and operations systems and centers that must disseminate and share SIGINT and communicate digitally creates a very dynamic situation.

The SIGINT effort depends heavily on a secure, reliable, and fast CIS architecture to receive SIGINT and all-source intelligence products and to pass collected data and SIGINT products and technical reports to the MAGTF and other users. Communications and information systems are also required for the C2 of SIGINT units and their integration with multidiscipline intelligence operations. Every mission and situation is unique, requiring some modifications to the CIS architecture supporting MAGTF SIGINT operations. Detailed planning and close coordination among the SIGINT units' CO or OICs, the MAGTF G-2/S-2 and G-6/S-6, and pertinent operational and intelligence organizations is critical to establishing reliable and effective SIGINT architecture.

See appendix B, Marine Corps SIGINT Equipment, of this publication for additional information on select communications and information systems resources pertinent to MAGTF SIGIN operations. Also, see MCWP 6-22, *Communications and Information Systems*, for a detailed review of MAGTF CIS and supporting tactics, techniques, and procedures.

6001. Basic MAGTF SIGINT CIS Requirements

a. Capability to Command and Control Subordinate Units

MAGTF SIGINT units must be capable of positive C2 of subordinate units and integration of its operations with broader MAGTF and external intelligence and operations C2. Traditionally, single-channel radio (SCR) and record message traffic have been used to support C2 of SIGIN units. In semistatic situations, secure electronic mail or the telephone may be the method of choice, while in highly fluid or mobile scenarios, cellular telephones, satellite communications (SATCOM), VHF, or HF radio may be used.

b. Ability to Receive and Transmit Collected Data and Information from Collection and DF Elements

The SIGINT architecture must provide connectivity among organic and supporting SIGINT collection or DF teams, SIGINT analysis and production centers, and supported MAGTF operations and intelligence centers. Requirements include the capability to receive and transmit collection files and reports digitally via fiber, wire, or radio (voice and data) in formats that are readily usable by the SIGINT and all-source intelligence analysts.

c. Ability to Provide Intelligence to the Supported Commander

The required SIGINT architecture must support the commander's intent, concepts of operation and intelligence, command relationships, and standing PIRs and IRs. The SIGINT CIS architecture must be capable of integrating SSU SCI-secure channels and C2 operations with the primary GENSER channels used by supported commanders throughout the MAGTF.

d. Ability to Share SIGINT Products and Technical Reports

The SIGINT architecture must provide the means to share products and reports with MAGTF all-source intelligence centers and with SIGINT and all-source JTF, other components, theater, and national intelligence centers. The traditional means for providing this capability are the SCI secure defense special security communication system (DSSCS) for record communications and operator's communications (OPSCOM) circuit for SIGINT analyst-to-analyst exchanges and coordination. These means are rapidly being replaced by—

- JWICS which provides interoperability of intelligence systems, access to intelligence data bases, and direct analyst-to-analyst exchange.
- National Security Agency Network (NSA-NET) which provides access to national-level SIGINT reports and data bases and electronic mail connectivity for SIGINT analyst-to-analyst exchanges and intelligence requests.

e. Ability to Receive and Disseminate SIGINT Indications and Warnings

A significant strength of SIGINT is its ability t provide time-sensitive I&W of the adversary's ac-

tions and intentions. This I&W intelligence is disseminated by a variety of means to include voice, record messages, tactical reports, electronic mail, and intelligence broadcasts. Having the capability to receive the information, recognizing the I&W intelligence as such, and possessing a method to disseminate this I&W intelligence to the affected units and decisionmakers are key to satisfying this requirement.

f. Ability to Receive SIGINT Broadcasts

For several years MAGTFs have possessed intelligence broadcast receivers capable of accessing select SIGINT broadcasts. The broadcast receivers currently being fielded and under development will allow MAGTFs to receive multiple channels of JTF, fleet, theater, and national intelligence broadcast data. This data includes all-source intelligence and SIGINT on enemy operations as well as friendly positional and other information. Effective planning, design, and integration of SCI and GENSER CIS and proper information management filtering, correlating, and tailoring prior to dissemination or display provide timely SIGINT reporting to supported commanders while preventing information overload.

6002. Notional MAGTF SIGINT Operational Architectures

a. MEF

Figure 6-1 depicts a notional SIGINT operational architecture for a fully deployed MEF. It shows a full complement of organic and supporting JTF other service components, theater, and nationa SIGINT capabilities.

Key architectural concepts include the following:

- SIGINT operations planning and management are centralized within the MAGTF G-2/S-2.

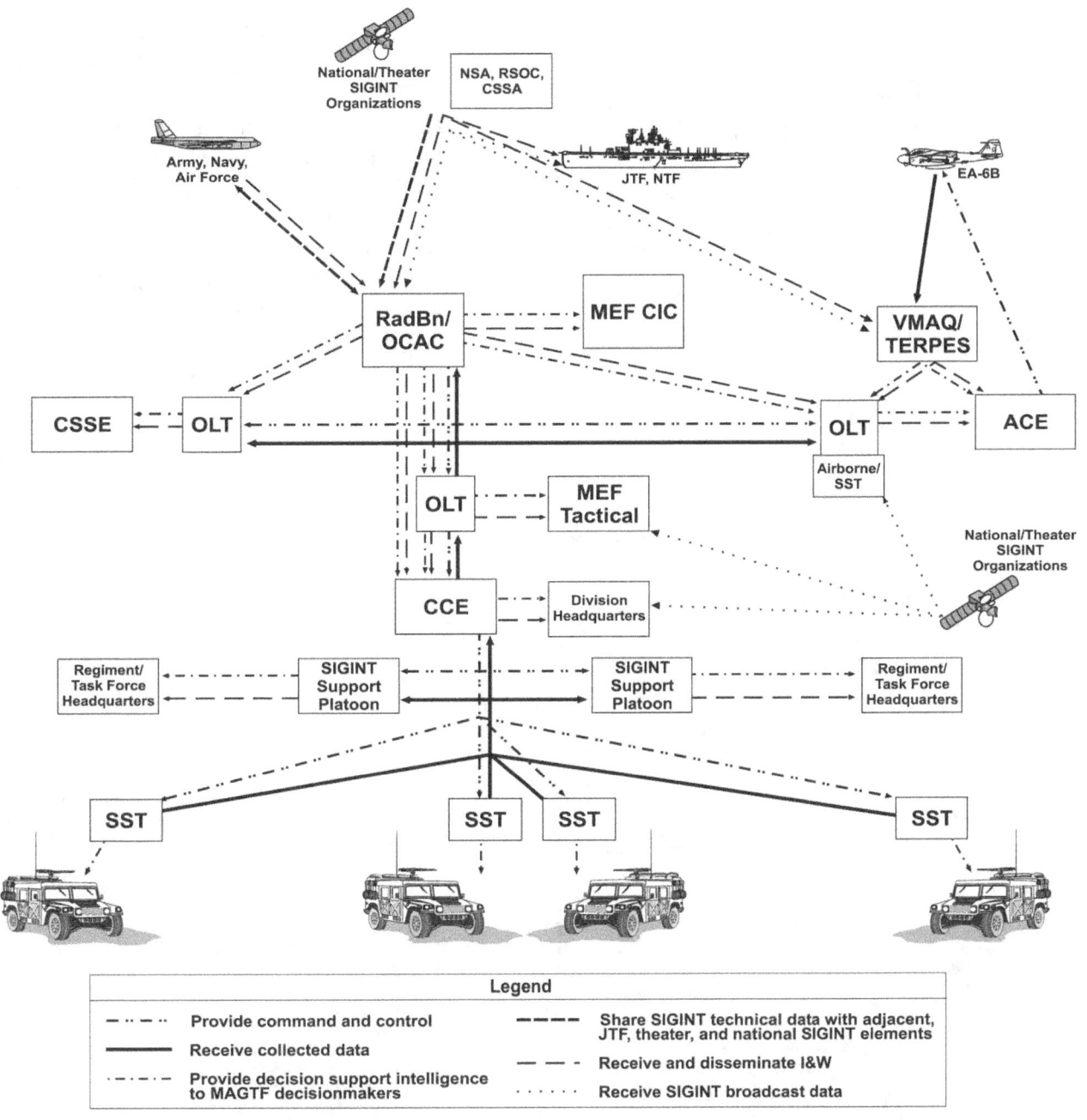

Figure 6-1. Notional MEF SIGINT Operational Architecture.

- RadBn OCAC is collocated with the G-2/ S-2 CIC and operates in general support of the MAGTF, with collection or DF teams collocated with forward-deployed MAGTF units.

- VMAQ TERPES is collocated with ACE headquarters and principally supports ACE operations.

- MAGTF CIC, RadBn OCAC, and TERPES maintain connectivity with appropriate external intelligence and SIGINT organizations.

b. MEF Lead Echelon

Figure 6-2 shows a notional operational architecture in support of the MEF lead echelon during its initial deployment and employment phases. SIGINT operations focus on the MEF as it deploys into the area of operations and builds its combat power.

Key architectural concepts include the following:

- SIGINT operations planning and management remain centralized within the MAGTF G-2/S-2, which is not yet within the area of operations.

- RadBn fly-in echelon is collocated with lead elements of the MAGTF G-2, with organi teams operating in GS of deployed elements. RadBn OCAC is collocated with the G-2/S-2 CIC.

- VMAQ TERPES is collocated with ACE headquarters and principally supports ACE operations.

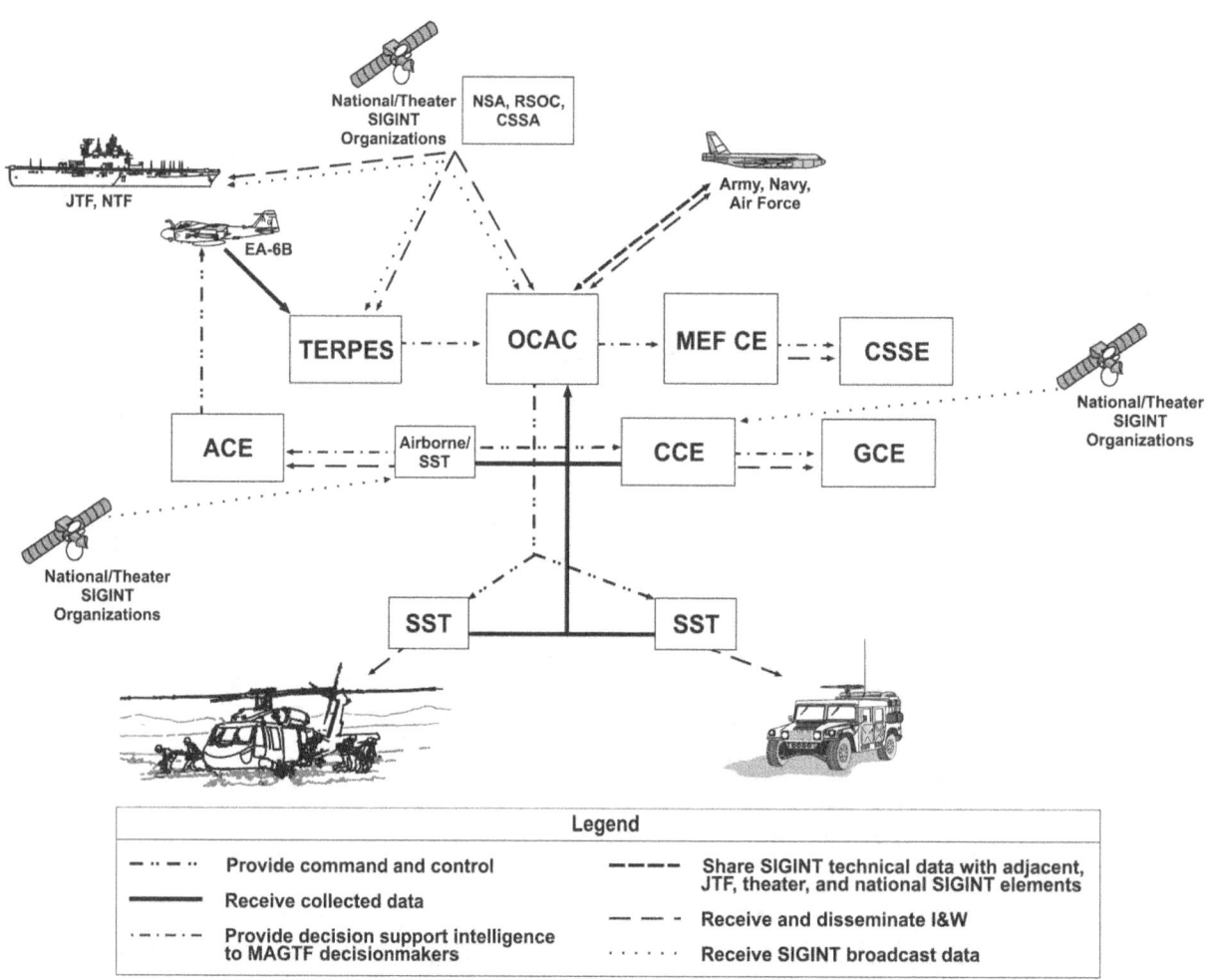

Figure 6-2. Notional MEF Lead Echelon SIGINT Operational Architecture.

- MAGTF CIC, RadBn OCAC, and TERPES maintain connectivity with appropriate external intelligence and SIGINT organizations.

c. MEU(SOC) CE Afloat

Figure 6-3 shows a notional operational architecture in support of a MEU(SOC) afloat. During such operations, MEU and ATF SIGINT capabilities and organizations generally collocate within the same afloat facilities (e.g., SSESs) integrate and share some systems operations. A critical component of this architecture is satisfactor voice and data ship-to-shore SCI communications between the MEU(SOC) command element and ashore SIGINT elements.

Key architectural concepts include the following:

- SIGINT operations planning and management are centralized in the MEU(SOC) S-2.
- RadBn SSU OCAC operates out of the SSES collocated with the S-2 CIC within the amphibious task force intelligence center (ATFIC). RadBn operates in general support of the MAGTF. Depending on the mission, RadBn collection and DF elements may operate in either general support of the MAGTF or direct support of elements operating ashore.
- MAGTF CIC and RadBn OCAC maintain connectivity with appropriate external intelligence and SIGINT organizations.

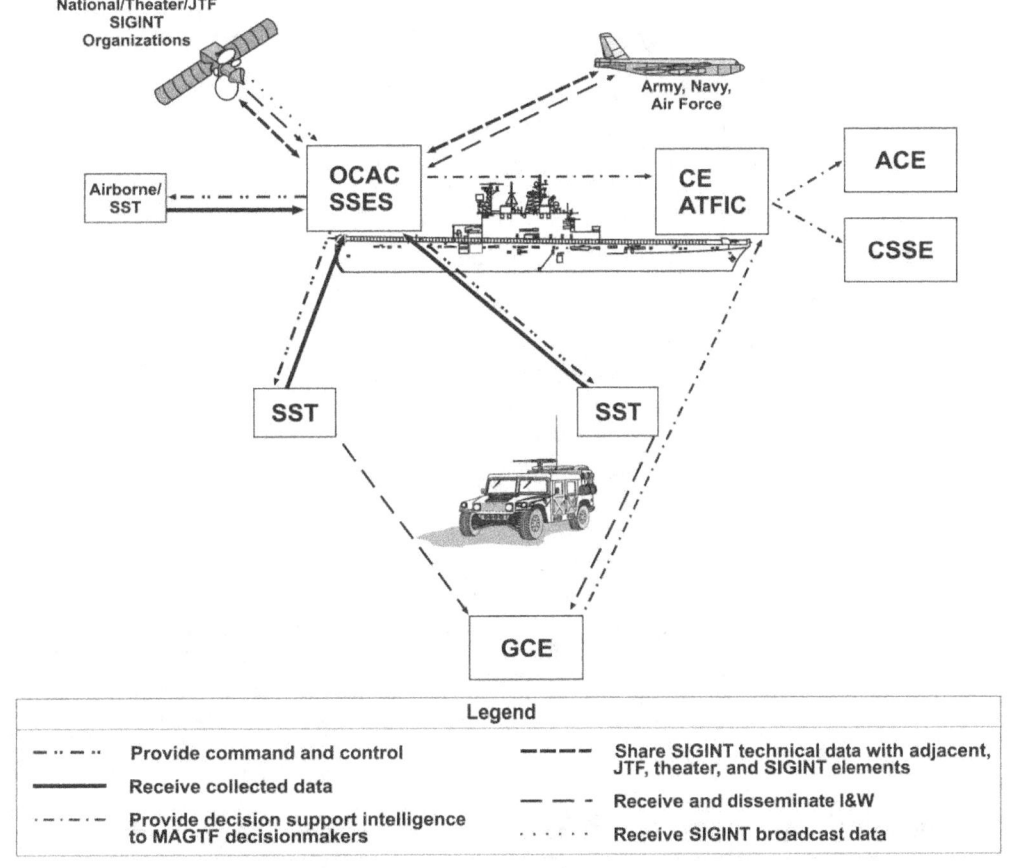

Figure 6-3. MEU(SOC) CE Afloat SIGINT Operational Architecture.

d. MEU(SOC) CE Ashore

Figure 6-4 depicts a notional operational architecture in support of a shore-based MEU(SOC) CE. The MEU(SOC) requires ship-to-shore SCI communications connectivity to continue exploiting external SIGINT capabilities and resources while minimizing the CIS and logistic footprints ashore.

Key architectural concepts include the following:

- SIGINT operations planning and C2 remain centralized within the MEU(SOC) S-2.

- The MAGTF RadBn SSU OCAC is collocated ashore with the S-2 CIC. Other SSU elements provide continued support from the amphibious task force intelligence center SSES.

- RadBn SSU normally will operate in GS of the MAGTF.

- MAGTF CIC and RadBn OCAC principal connectivity with appropriate external intelligence and SIGINT organizations is via the amphibious task force intelligence center SSES.

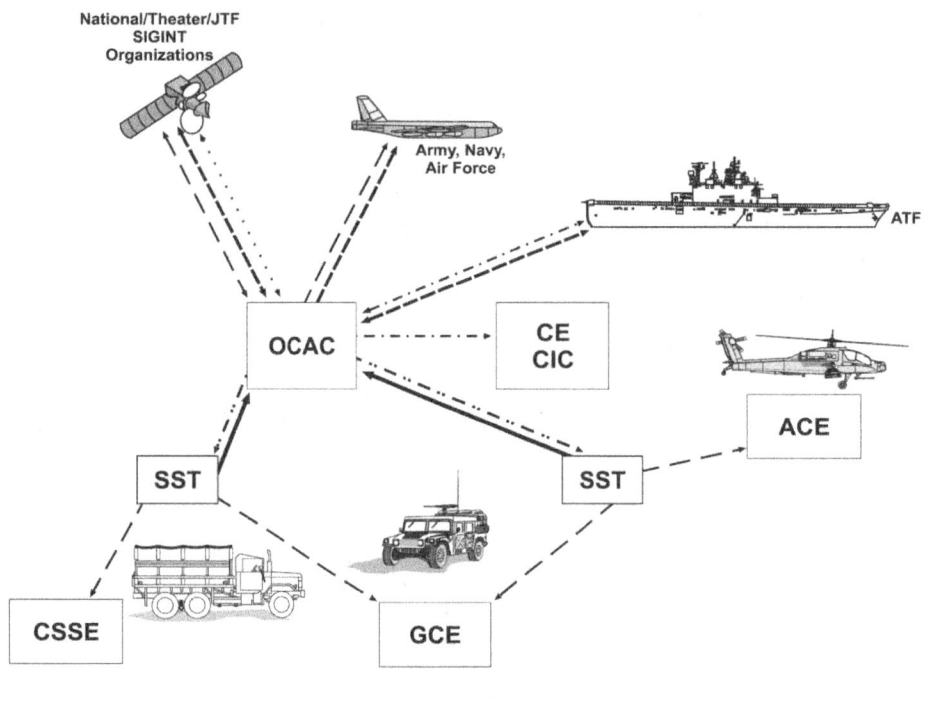

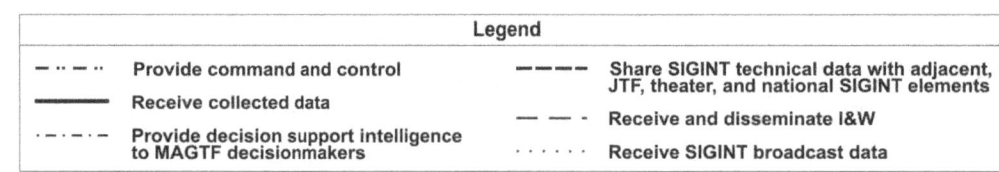

Figure 6-4. MEU(SOC) CE Ashore SIGINT Operational Architecture.

6003. Planning Consideration

The following are key CIS requirements and planning considerations in support of MAGTF SIGINT operations.

- Add the MAGTF CE, RadBn SSU, VMAQ TERPES, and other MAGTF elements to appropriate addressee indicator groups (AIGs) to receive pertinent JTF, theater, and national intelligence and SIGINT products.
- Obtain and activate SCI plain language addresses for MAGTF CE, RadBn SSU, and other MAGTF elements as appropriate.
- Determine and coordinate radio nets, supporting frequencies, and procedures for—
  - MAGTF external SIGINT operations.
  - MAGTF internal SIGINT operations.
  - Intelligence broadcasts.
  - Retransmission sites.
  - Routine and time-sensitive operations.
- Obtain authority and establish procedures for the sanitization of SIGINT products, reports, and other information.
- Determine and coordinate wire communications, to include telephones.
- Determine and coordinate SCI and GENSER LANs and WANs and unique intelligence networks information systems requirements (e.g., hardware, software, internet protocol addresses).
- Determine and coordinate SCI-courier requirements and operations.
- Integrate RadBn SSU and VMAQ CIS operations with those of other MAGTF and pertinent JTF and other components intelligence and reconnaissance units (e.g., mutual support, cueing).
- Integrate RadBn SSU, SSE, and SST, and VMAQ TERPES communications with collocated GCE, ACE, CSSE, and other MAGTF elements to—

  - Provide time-sensitive I&W and non-codeword (NCW) SIGINT reporting.
  - Coordinate with maneuver forces.
  - Support targeting.
  - Support force protection.
- Coordinate SIGINT CIS and dissemination operations and procedures with allied and coalition forces.
- Coordinate SCI and SIGINT CIS activation and restoration priorities and procedures.
- Determine unique COMSEC material system (CMS) requirements for SIGINT and SCI communications.
- Determine communications requirements between TSCIFs and mobile SCIFs and supporting security forces.

6004. SIGINT Communications

The SIGINT CIS architecture for any given operation is dynamic. Specific theater, JTF, or MAGTF reference documents include—

- CSPs developed for various OPLANs.
- Combatant commanders intelligence, CIS, and SIGINT tactics, techniques, and procedures (TTPs).
- Annexes B (intelligence), C (operations), and K (communications) of an OPORD.
- Appendix 2 (SIGINT) to annex B of an OPORD.

The MAGTF mission, threat signals environment, friendly concepts of operations and intelligence, and supporting task organization and command relationships influence which communications nets are established.

The following information addresses importan aspects of systems and technical architectures in support of MAGTF SIGINT operations.

a. MAGTF Command Element SIGINT Communications Nets

Figure 6-5 shows aspects of a notional CIS architecture for the MEF CIC. The following key SIGINT communications nets terminate within the MAGTF CE CIC or RadBn SSU.

(1) MAGTF DSSCS or Special Intelligence Communications Net External (HF). The DSSCS provides the MAGTF commander with a secure data communications channel for the exchange of SCI information and the receipt of record communications. The path is provided by the supported commander, and the terminal equipment and personnel are provided by the RadBn SSU. Key net participants include—

- The MAGTF CE via the RadBn SSU's special security communications element.
- Commander, joint task force (CJTF).
- Commander, amphibious task force (CATF).
- Other theater and national organizations.

(2) MAGTF Critical Communications Net (UHF-SATCOM/VHF). The critical communications (CRITICOMM) net provides the MAGTF commander communications with adjacent service cryptologic and other SIGINT and JTF elements and theater cryptologic support groups The path is provided by the supported commander, and the terminal equipment and personnel are provided by the RadBn SSCT. Key net participants include—

- MAGTF CE via the RadBn or SSU special security communications element.
- JTF.
- Adjacent headquarters.
- Theater and national intelligence or SIGINT agencies.

(3) Theater Cryptologic Support Net (HF/ UHF-SATCOM). Theater cryptologic support net provides for rapid exchange of cryptologic information with the SIGINT elements of other organizations. The path is provided by the supported commander, and the terminal equipment is provided by the RadBn/SSU. Key participants include—

- RadBn OCAC.
- Adjacent service cryptologic elements.
- JTF or ATF SIGINT agencies.
- Theater and national SIGINT agencies.

(4) Tactical Receive Equipment and Related Applications Program Data Dissemination System. The TRE and related applications program data dissemination system (TDDS) broadcast provides I&W and global surveillance information in time for sensor cueing. Data is forwarded from sensor to communications gateways or relays for dissemination to worldwide military users via geosynchronous UHF satellite links. TDDS data sources include national and tactical sensor systems. Participants include the MAGTF CE CIC or SSU OCAC and other JTF, theater, and national intelligence centers and agencies.

(5) Tactical Information Broadcast Service. The tactical information broadcast service (TIBS) provides near-real-time intelligence from an open network of interactive participants using multiple sensors and sources. The TIBS broadcast uses UHF SATCOM assets for network operation and for the relay of out-of-theater specific information into the tactical users' areas of operation. TIBS participants include a wide variety of national and Service airborne, surface, and subsurface intelligence platforms. The broadcast will terminate in the MAGTF CE CIC or SSU OCAC.

(6) Tactical Intelligence Net. Tactical intelligence (TACINTEL) net is an automated, high speed data link for transmission and reception of SCI (data and voice) among SIGINT collection and production units during amphibious operations. Key participants include naval expeditionary force (NEF) and ATF SIGINT centers (within the SSES) and the RadBn and SSU OCAC.

(7) MAGTF-Internal Special Intelligence Communications Net (VHF/UHF/SHF). Special intelligence communications (SPINTCOMM) net provides the MAGTF commander with secure SCI communications with subordinate division or wing commanders through their organic SSCT.

The path is provided by the supported commander, and the terminal equipment and personnel are provided by the RadBn SSU or SSCT.

(8) TROJAN SPIRIT II Net. The Trojan Spirit II net (C and Ku band SATCOM) receives and disseminates intelligence information over a special-purpose satellite system. Key participants include the MAGTF CE CIC, RadBn SSU OCAC, amphibious task force intelligence center SSES and various external intelligence agencies and organizations.

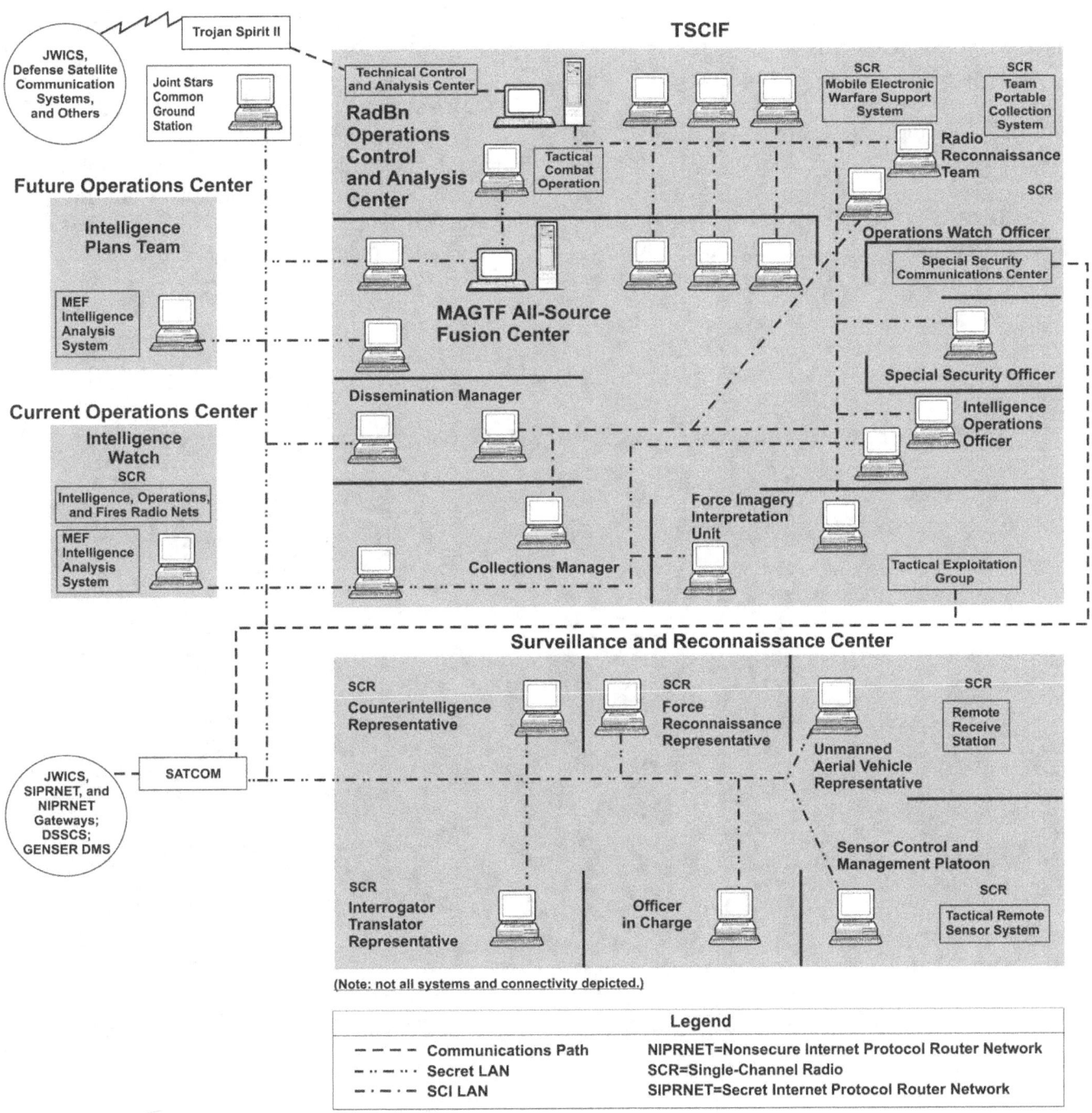

Figure 6-5. MEF CE CIC Communications and Information Systems Architecture.

b. Radio Battalion SIGINT Support Unit Internal Communications Nets

Figure 6-6 shows key aspects of the CIS architecture for the internal operations of the RadBn SSU. The following key communications nets terminate within the RadBn SSU OCAC.

(1) Command and Control Net (HF/VHF).
The RadBn SSU C2 net provides the battalion commander or detachment OIC with C2 of subordinate elements. The path, equipment, and personnel are provided by the RadBn. Key net participants include the RadBn SSU OCAC and deployed collection and DF, EA, and RRT teams.

(2) Collection and Reporting Net (UHF-SATCOM/HF/VHF).
The collection and reporting net provides C2 and SIGINT reporting net for RadBn SSU collection operations. Key participants include the OCAC and deployed collection and DF teams.

(3) Electronic Attack Control Net (VHF).
The EA control net provides direction and control of RadBn EA teams and assets. The path, equipment, and personnel are provided by the RadBn SSU. Key participants include the OCAC and deployed MEWSS and EA teams.

(4) Direction Finding Flash Net (VHF).
The DF flash net provides the DF control station with a means of broadcasting DF flashes to DF teams. The path, equipment, and personnel are provided by the RadBn. Key participants include the OCAC's DF control and deployed collection and DF teams.

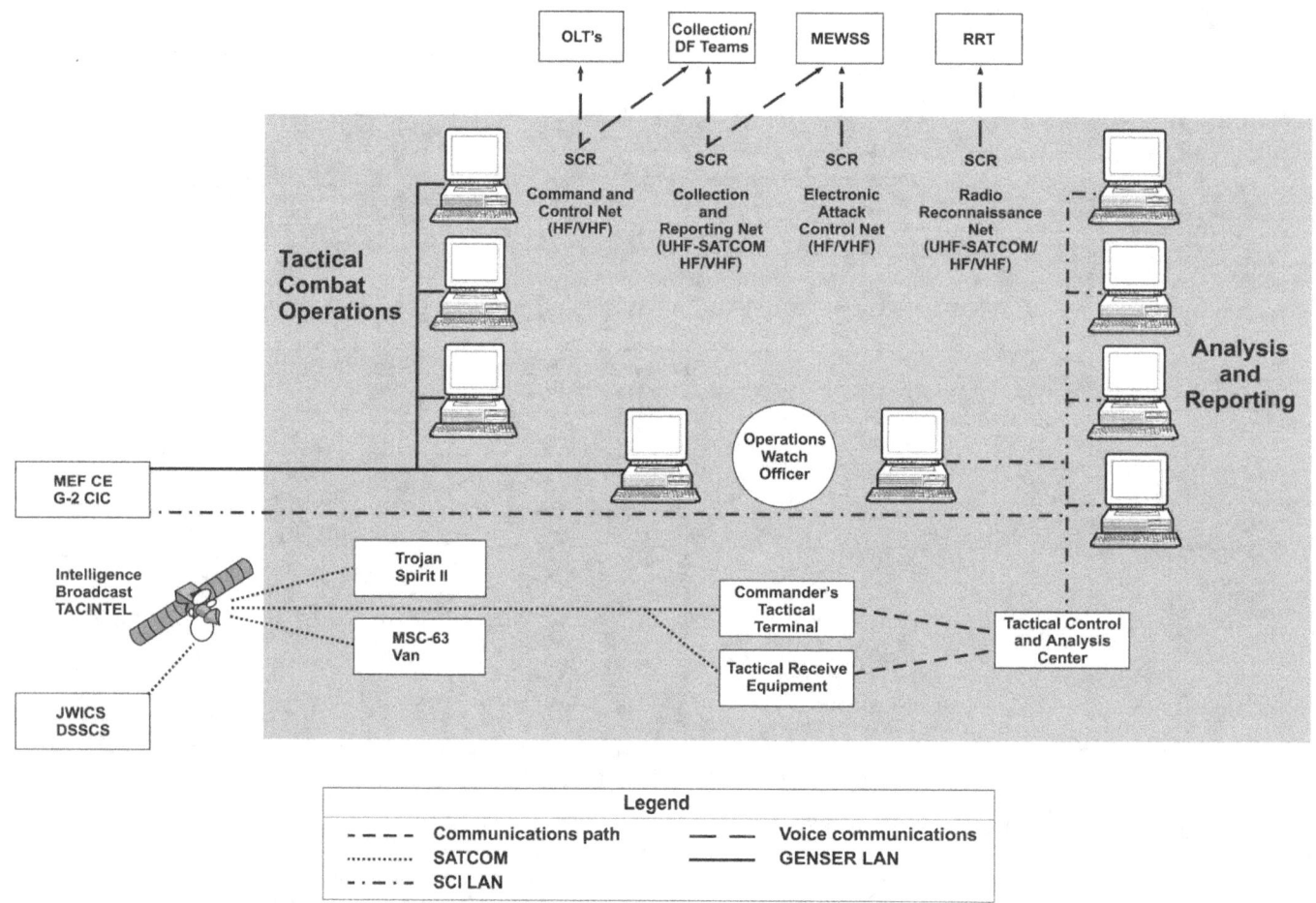

Figure 6-6. RadBn SSU Operations Control and Analysis Center Communications and Information Systems.

(5) Direction Finding Report Net (VHF). The DF report net provides reporting from DF outstations to the OCAC DF control. Path, equipment, and personnel are provided by the RadBn SSU.

(6) Direction Finding Data Net (VHF). The DF data net exchanges DF information between the deployed collection and DF team and the OCAC DF control. The path, equipment, and personnel are provided by the RadBn.

(7) Mission Equipment Control Data Link Net (UHF). The mission equipment control dat link (MECDL) net provides the means to control, coordinate, and monitor the mission equipment of MEWSS teams. This net is used for internal MEWSS operations and for interface and coordination with the Army intelligence and EW common sensor systems.

(8) Tasking and Reporting Net (VHF) The tasking and reporting net provides a means for the RadBn to task deployed collection teams and to report SIGINT information.

(9) Radio Reconnaissance Command Net (UHF-Tactical Satellite/HF) The radio reconnaissance command net provides the means to command and control deployed RRTs and their reporting of SIGINT collection and DF reports to the RadBn SSU OCAC.

c. Marine Tactical Electronic Warfare Squadron Communications Nets

Figure 6-7 shows key aspects of the CIS architecture for VMAQ TERPES operations. The following key SIGINT communications nets terminate within VMAQ operations or TERPES elements.

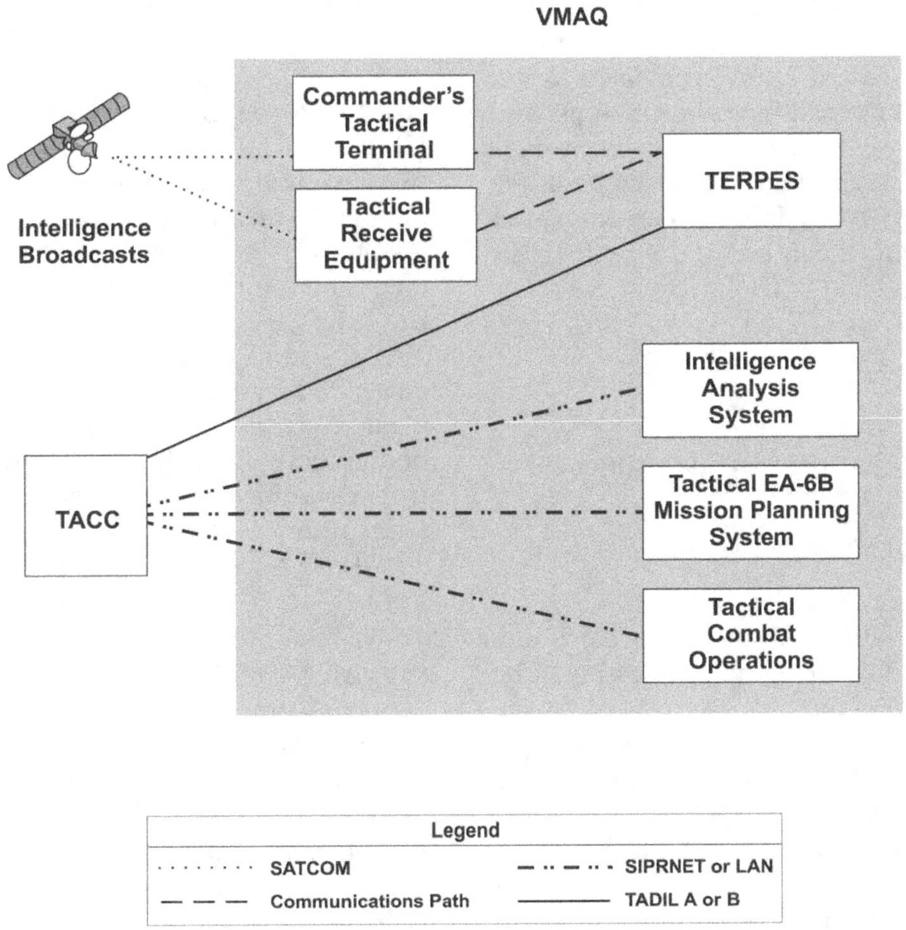

Figure 6-7. VMAQ Operations Center and TERPES Communications and Information Systems.

(1) Aviation Combat Element Command Net (HF). The ACE command net provides a means for the ACE commander to exercise command and coordinate subordinate units' administrative and logistic functions. Composition includes ACE headquarters, MAG detachments Marine air control group or detachment, and independent squadrons or battalions.

(2) Aviation Combat Element Intelligence Net (VHF/HF/UHF). The ACE intelligence ne provides a means for rapid collection and dissemination of intelligence between the ACE headquarters and subordinate units. Composition includes the ACE headquarters, the TACC, MAGs or squadrons headquarters, the tactical air operations center (TAOC), direct air support center (DASC), TERPES, and others as appropriate.

(3) Tactical Digital Information Link A (HF/UHF). Tactical digital information link A (TADIL-A), also called Link-11, is used to exchange tactical data in real time among ships, aircraft, and shore sites. TADIL-A messages provide navigational data, surface and subsurface tracks, and operational orders. TADIL-A is an encrypted half-duplex system. It can be used on either H single- or dual-sideband or UHF frequencies.

There are two data rates:

- Fast, at 2250 bits per second (bps) which is the most used data rate.
- Slow, at 1364 bps.

TADIL-A is available within the United State Navy, Air Force, Marine Corps, and Army. The MAGTF's C2 nodes that can use TADIL-A are the TAOC and the TACC. The exchange of digital information by TADIL-A is accomplished by net-configured participating units (PUs) under the control of a net control station (NCS). A net can be composed of as few as two PUs (e.g., TERPES, via the TACC, and the TAOC).

(4) Tactical Digital Information Link B (Multichannel Radio). TADIL-B, multichannel radio (MUX), (also known as Link-11B) is a full-duplex, point-to-point, encrypted system that simultaneously exchanges tactical data between two units capable of TADIL-B at a rate of 600 1200, and 2400 bps. TADIL-B messages provide navigational data, surface and subsurface tracks, and operational orders. It may use VHF, UHF, SHF, and ground mobile force-SATCOM MUX systems. Additionally, TADIL-B can also be exchanged over wire. TADIL-B is used by the United States Air Force, Army, and Marine Corps. MAGTF C2 nodes with TADIL-B capability are the TACC, TAOC, and Marine air traffic control detachment (MATCD). Participants on a TADIL-B network, such as TERPES, are called reporting units (RUs). Some RUs are capable of simultaneously linking with several other RUs. Those units that can redistribute the information re ceived from one RU to another RU are called forwarding reporting units (e.g., TACC and TAOC).

(5) Tactical Digital Information Link C (UHF). TADIL-C, also called Link-4A, is used by the North Atlantic Treaty Organization (NATO) and the United States Armed Forces. TADIL-C is an unencrypted, computer-to-computer digital information link that operates in the UHF frequency range at 5000 bps. The TADIL-C link is between a controlling unit and a controlled tactical aircraft. TADIL-C is a valuable means for providing radar track correlated symbology both up to the aircraft and, in the case of two-way transmissions, back down to the controlling agency. The MAGTF TAOC uses the TADIL-C for one-way and two-way links to control F-14, F/A-18, EA-6B, and S-3 aircraft.

(6) Voice Product Net (UHF). The voice product net (VPN) provides a communications means for forwarding nondigital intelligence information to other intelligence and operations elements. Key MAGTF participants include the TACC, TAOC, EA-6B, and TERPES, as well as other MAGT external platforms (e.g., Rivet Joint, Compass Call, EP-3).

Chapter 7

Planning and Operations

The purpose of SIGINT operations is to develop intelligence on the enemy's capabilities, intent, and operations by exploiting the enemy's use of communication, radars, and electronic systems.

Section I. SIGINT Functional Planning

Detailed planning must precede actual SIGINT operations to take advantage of the wealth of information available on the adversary's signals emanations and operations.

7101. SIGINT Concept of Operations

SIGINT operations must support the commander's intent, concept of operations, and the supporting concept of intelligence operations.

Questions that must be answered to develop the SIGINT concept of operations include the following:

ı What is the MAGTF area of operations (AO) and area of interest (AI)?

ı What is the MAGTF concept of operations, task organization, and main and supporting efforts? Does the friendly concept of operations allow for fixed-site SIGINT collection and DF operations, mobile collection and DF operations, or both?

ı What are the standing PIRs and IRs? Which have been tasked to SIGINT units? What specific information is the commander most interested in (e.g., enemy air operations, enemy ground operations, friendly force protection, target battle damage assessment [BDA], or enemy future intentions)?

ı What is the MAGTF force protection concept of operations?

ı What is the MAGTF concept of fire support? How will MAGTF target development and target intelligence be conducted?

ı What are the SIGINT and intelligence concepts of operations of other JTF components, the JTF, and theater resources? What are the task organization and command or support relationships for all other MAGTF intelligence and reconnaissance units?

ı How can shipboard SIGINT assets and other JTF, theater, and national SIGINT assets be integrated and employed to support MAGTF operations?

7102. Enemy Characteristics

Intelligence operations focus on the enemy. Prior to commencing SIGINT operations, MAGTF intelligence personnel must learn as much as they can about the following enemy C2 CIS practices.

a. Size and Composition of Enemy Forces

ı What threat forces are within the MAGTF AO and AI?

ı What are the enemy's centers of gravity and critical vulnerabilities?

ı Is this a large enemy force organized along conventional military lines or a small, loosely knit guerrilla or unconventional military force?

b. Enemy Command and Control and Supporting Communications and Information Systems

ı What and where are the enemy's critical C2 nodes and what are their vulnerabilities?

ı What types and categories of communications nets and networks are used by the enemy?

ı What echelons of command do the communications nets and networks serve?

ı What are the associated communications and noncommunications electronic emitters?

ı What are the tactics, techniques, and procedures used for enemy CIS operations? How do they relate to various threat functional activities?

ı How is information transferred among the enemy's units and command echelons?

ı Does the enemy employ communications emitters at all levels of command or does it rely on communications means less exploitable by SIGINT (e.g., fiber, wire, and messenger)?

c. Emitter Technical Data

Effective SIGINT operations require extensive technical information on the enemy's CIS resources and operations. See table 7-1 for key threat emitter technical data requirements.

7103. Topography

Terrain, physical obstructions, and vegetation in the area of operations have a major effect on the employment of SIGINT resources and their ability to exploit enemy signals. Proper placement of SIGINT collection and DF assets is essential for effective reception of adversary emanations. Several factors affect reception quality.

a. Target Frequencies

Many of the frequency ranges and power levels in use by the world's military and paramilitary forces require line-of-sight (LOS) or near-LOS paths from transmitter to receiver. Generally, the higher

Table 7-1. Emitter Technical Data.

Aspect	Technical and Operational Characteristics
Communications Operations and Emitters	
Frequency range and use	HF, VHF, UHF, etc.
Call sign use	Rota, random, etc.
Transmitter power	Hearability, SIGINT collection, and DF location requirements
Emission type	Single, multichannel, spread spectrum, frequency hopping, burst, etc.
Signal type	Analog or digital
Modulation	AM, FM, PCM, etc.
Cryptologic system	Public, private key, none
System type	Voice, data, teletype, facsimile, video, combinations of some or all
Language use	Dialect, written, or voice
Miscellaneous	Communication procedures, emissions control practices, use of deception, security systems, etc.
Noncommunications Operations and Emitters	
Location	Fixed, mobile
Platform	Air, ship, vehicle, fixed-installation
Associated C2 node or weapon system	Command post, type of weapon system
Frequency range	Band of operation
Modulation characteristics	Pulse duration, pulse repetition frequency, etc.
Transmitter power	Effective radiated power, effective range
Purpose of function	Jamming, surveillance, targeting, C2, fire control, etc.

the frequency used, the greater the LOS influence and the more critical the accurate placement of SIGINT collection and DF equipment. Lower frequencies (particularly those below 30 MHz) generally do not require LOS paths. Consequently, the placement of SIGINT collection and DF sites to exploit these frequencies may be located at greater distances from the target transmitters.

b. Power Output

The power output of a transmitter is an important factor in receiving the signal. To intercept some low-powered signals, SIGINT collection and DF assets must be located closer to the adversary's transmitter, often requiring SIGINT collection and DF teams to either collocate with or closely follow forward MAGTF combat units.

c. Antennas

If the targeted adversary's system uses highly directional antennas, as do many multichannel systems, the SIGINT collection and DF site must be placed within the adversary's antenna radiating pattern.

7104. Planning Responsibilities

Primary staff responsibility for SIGINT operations planning lies with the G-2/S-2. The G-2/S-2 responsibilities are—

- Preparing integrated, multidiscipline intelligence and reconnaissance operations, to include supporting SIGINT plans, orders, annexes, and appendices.
- Coordinating with the G-3/S-3 to ensure—
  - Planned SIGINT effort will support the concept of operations and scheme of maneuver.
  - SIGINT and EW operations are effectively prioritized and integrated.
  - Adequate site placement and security for SIGINT collection elements is provided.
- Coordinating with the G-6/S-6 officer for CIS support to the SIGINT elements, including circuits and networks access, frequency assignment, equipment, and call signs.

- Acting as liaison with SIGINT agencies and units external to the MAGTF.
- Coordinating with the G-4/S-4 to ensure adequate logistics support of SIGINT elements (e.g., transportation and maintenance of SIGINT units' unique equipment).

7105. Coordination of SIGINT Operations

a. Internal Coordination

Internal MAGTF SIGINT requirements must be coordinated with maneuver, fires, electronic warfare, force protection, and CIS requirements. This coordination may occur within the EWCC under G-3/S-3 staff cognizance, within the CIC, or within the OCAC, depending upon the task organization and C2 and support relationships in effect. Additionally, collection and DF team movements and locations must be coordinated with the MAGTF's tactical movements to ensure continuous support without interference.

These efforts are accomplished through planning and close coordination among the following MAGTF staff officers:

- MAGTF G-2/S-2, the intelligence operations officer, and the intelligence battalion commander.
- SIO, MAGTF AFC OIC, collections officer, SARC OIC, and the dissemination manager.
- MAGTF G-3/S-3 future and current operations officers, C2W officer, and EWO.
- MAGTF G-6/S-6.
- GCE, ACE, and CSSE staff officers.
- RadBn SSU and VMAQ TERPES COs and OICs.

b. External Coordination

(1) Higher Headquarters and External Organizations. The MAGTF G-2/S-2 and all SIGINT planners must coordinate SIGINT operations, activities, and requirements with DIRNSA. Accordingly, a continuous exchange of data and information is required. This requires JWICS access and special security communications circuits for the exchange of SIGINT technical data and intelligence information.

(2) Adjacent and Area SIGINT Activities. MAGTF SIGINT activities must be coordinated with other SIGINT activities within the joint operations area and theater to reduce duplication and to ensure maximum use of available assets and mutual support. For example, an NSG-fixed site outside the MAGTF tactical operations area could be conducting SIGINT collection and DF against targets within the MAGTF area of responsibility. With proper planning and coordination, external SIGINT assets of the combatant commander, JTF, and other components can provide SIGINT support to the MAGTF (e.g., product reporting, exchanges of technical information), allowing organic MAGTF SIGINT resources to focus on critical targets.

Section II. SIGINT Operational Planning

This section provides a general description of the SIGINT planning cycle and activities to enable an understanding and appreciation for the SIGINT effort as a whole. No attempt is made to provide technical details for SIGINT processing. The SIGINT cycle is in concert with the following six phases of the intelligence cycle (see MCWP 2-1 for additional information on the intelligence cycle and intelligence planning).

7201. Planning and Direction

The planning and direction phase of the intelligence cycle consists of those activities which identify and prioritize pertinent IRs and provide the means for satisfying them. Intelligence planning and direction is a continuous function and a command responsibility. The commander directs the intelligence effort; the intelligence officer manages this effort based upon the commander's intent, designation of PIRs, and specific guidance provided during the planning process. The intelligence planning and direction functions are—

- Requirements development.
- Requirements management.
- Collections management.
- Production management.
- Dissemination management.
- Intelligence support structure.
- Supervision of the intelligence effort.

SIGINT planning is performed in concert with overall intelligence planning. It consists of those activities that identify pertinent IRs which have been tasked to SIGINT units and then provides the means for satisfying those IRs. SIGINT planning and direction is a continuous function that requires close interaction between the G-2/S-2 and SIGINT unit planners.

SIGINT planning and direction objectives include—

- Identifying intelligence requirements tasked to SIGINT elements.
- Preparing a SIGINT operations plan, to include integral SIGINT collection, production, and dissemination plans.
- Planning and establishing the SIGINT support system (e.g., CIS, logistics).
- Issuing orders and tasking to SIGINT units.
- Supervising and coordinating the SIGINT operations.

The selection of a particular source of information or intelligence discipline to fulfill a given intelligence requirement is an important decision. SIGINT is a valuable source of information, and an effective, dynamic SIGINT operations plan must be developed to maximize the effectiveness of the SIGINT effort. With the multitude of threat signals being transmitted, the collection plan must be carefully constructed to collect and exploit enemy signals that are most likely to provide the necessary intelligence data. Additionally, the SIGINT production and dissemination plans must effectively support unique SIGINT and all-source intelligence operations requirements and operations.

a. Mission Planning

Based on the commander's PIRs and IRs, the G-2/S-2 determines those ICRs which are applicable to and have the potential to be satisfied by the organic SIGINT collection effort. The G-2/S-2 incorporates these ICRs into the overall intelligence collection plan and issues mission tasking and guidance to the RadBn OIC, ACE G-2/S-2, and other attached or supporting SIGINT units. Additionally, SIGINT taskings from the joint force commander (JFC) and supplemental taskings from DIRNSA will need to be assessed by the G-2/S-2 and incorporated if possible into MAGTF SIGINT operations (refer to USSID 4 for additional information regarding DIRNSA supplemental tasking).

b. Mission Management

SIGINT mission management is the unit commander's supervision of collection, processing, production, and dissemination efforts. Proper mission management requires centralized control of SIGINT assets at the MAGTF command element level. The OCAC (for RadBn SSUs) and the TERPES section (for VMAQ) provide this centralized control for the their respective SIGINT efforts. Collection and DF elements are usually positioned throughout the MAGTF's operations area based on the MAGTF's focus of effort, scheme of maneuver, hearability of enemy signals, and security of SIGINT units. Air SIGINT operations in support of both ACE and MAGTF requirements will be planned and incorporated in the supporting air tasking order (ATO). SIGINT unit commanders and planners must ensure that coverage is complete, that assets are gainfully employed or redirected, and that SIGINT reporting (and supporting CIS support) is effective. Collection tasks must be analyzed to determine if they can be met or if new collection or analysis efforts are required. The collection, direction finding, and analysis and production efforts must be supervised, integrated with all-source intelligence operations, and evaluated to ensure mission effectiveness.

7202. Collection

During collection, organic, attached, and supporting SIGINT elements collect and deliver information to the appropriate processing or production element (e.g., OCAC or TERPES). In some instances (e.g., immediate threat) the information will be delivered directly to the local commander for immediate action.

a. COMINT Collection

COMINT collection is performed using equipment that intercepts adversary communications signals. Simple signals (e.g., unencrypted single-channel voice) can be received by ordinary receivers. More complicated signals or those that are encrypted require more sophisticated equipment to fully exploit the signals for their intelligence value (i.e., external SIGINT processing and production centers such as the RSOCs or NSA).

Initially, a concentrated intercept search, signals analysis, and target development program is carried out to catalog the electromagnetic environment and identify the desired threat SOIs. In many cases, prior knowledge of some technical characteristics, such as in RSOC or CSSA data bases, will enhance and streamline the MAGTF's COMINT search effort. When SOIs are acquired that are readily exploitable, SIGINT collection operators prepare a gist of the transmission. Recording of the entire intercepted signal using tape recorders may also occur.

Multichannel transmissions are first divided by SIGINT operators into their component parts or separate channels and then processed channel by channel. The acquired data (e.g., logs, gists, data files, page-prints, tapes) are rapidly assessed against standing PIRs for items of immediate tactical intelligence value and reported in accordance with reporting and dissemination criteria to—

ı Designated commanders.
ı OCAC or TERPES production elements for detailed analysis and reporting.
ı MAGTF AFC for all-source analysis and production.

b. Direction Finding

Radio DF uses electronic equipment to obtain the locations of adversary emitters by determining the direction of arrival or the time difference of arrival of the radio waves. In ideal conditions, direction finders are arrayed in a network along a predetermined baseline consisting of at least three collection and DF stations, one of which acts as net control. The DF sites must be placed carefully so that all stations can hear the target SOI and mutually support the mission.

Close coordination between collection and DF sites and the OCAC is required for a responsive DF effort. RadBn SSU DF results are then reported, either manually or via automated means, to the OCAC for follow-on intelligence exploitation and reporting.

c. ELINT Collection and Direction Finding

Although few in numbers, the RadBn MEWSS product improvement program (PIP) (AN/MLQ-36A) provides for the automated search, acquisition, identification, and a single DF line of bearing of radars and other noncommunications emitters. Mission management, reporting, and dissemination are handled similarly to COMINT DF operations.

Additionally, in support of its strike escort mission, VMAQ elements collect ELINT information that can be used by MAGTF intelligence producers such as the MAGTF AFC and OCAC. Technical capabilities within the EA-6B's ELINT collection system allow for DF operations to occur from a single aircraft. Acquired signals are recorded and then provided to the TERPES section for postmission analysis, production, and reporting.

7203. Processing and Exploitation

The following processing and exploitation functions are used to convert collected raw information into a form suitable for SIGINT production.

a. Traffic Analysis

Traffic analysis is the study of all characteristics of communications except encrypted texts. Call signs, frequencies, times of transmission, cryptographic indicators, precedence, and message lengths are examples of these characteristics. These characteristics are called externals and are compiled and sorted primarily for the purpose of reconstructing the adversary's communication structure and organization. This information yields valuable electronic order of battle data and other information. With on-line communication encryption systems becoming widely used by potential adversaries, traffic analysis becomes an increasingly difficult function.

b. Cryptanalysis

Cryptanalysis is the study of encrypted signals, data, and texts to determine their plain language equivalents. The capability to read the adversary's encrypted communications is obviously valuable. The RadBns' limited cryptanalysis capability depends on the sophistication of the target's encryption system and the availability of specialized equipment and software resources from NSA.

c. Linguistic Analysis

Linguistic analysis is the transcription and translation of foreign language intercepts into English. This analysis starts at the collection site upon interception. Messages of considerable length require more time and are usually transcribed and translated in the OCAC. Marines are trained in a wide variety of languages for this task, but augmentation by external sources (e.g., native and/or contract linguists) may be required in order to satisfy all requirements.

d. Signal Analysis

Signal analysis consists of working with all types of signals (e.g., COMINT, ELINT, pro forma) to identify, isolate, reduce to pure form, and exploit acquired SOIs. The signal analyst must be well trained and possess the proper electronic and software support tools to be effective.

e. ELINT Analysis

The location of early warning, surveillance, and fire control radars can provide a general trace of the adversary's forward battle positions and locations of key C2 and fire control nodes and weapons systems. Medium-range and counterweapons radar identification provides order of battle information since these systems are organic to specific adversary units.

Identification and location of air defense radars provide information on the disposition of the adversary's air defense systems and their threat to strike, close air support, and assault support aircraft. Following the reporting of any I&W information to tactical decisionmakers, technical data and detailed ELINT information is forwarded to the OCAC or to the TERPES section for further analysis, production, and reporting.

7204. Production

Production is the conversion of raw information into SIGINT product reports through the evaluation, integration, and interpretation of the information derived during the processing and exploitation effort. The results of the analysis are correlated by SIGINT analysts and reporters to form the basis for SIGINT reports. These reports are provided directly to tactical commanders when appropriate, to the G-2/S-2 for the further analysis and production of all-source intelligence, and to the staff sections for future operations planning.

SIGINT production planning and management are closely coordinated with all-source intelligence production planning and management to—

- Determine the scope, content, and format for each product.
- Develop a plan and schedule for the development of products.
- Assign priorities among the various SIGINT product requirements.
- Allocate SIGINT processing, exploitation, and production resources.
- Integrate production efforts with all-source collection and dissemination activities.

The production goal is the effective and efficient use of limited resources while focusing on established SIGINT priorities.

a. Evaluation

SIGINT analysts evaluate the raw SIGINT information to determine its pertinence to intelligence requirements. Further evaluation is made to judge the reliability and accuracy of the information and to isolate significant elements.

b. Integration

The information derived from traffic analysis, cryptanalysis, linguistic analysis, signal analysis, ELINT analysis, and radio DF must be fully integrated into a fused SIGINT product to develop a complete SIGINT picture. Concurrently, integration of SIGINT processing and production with ongoing MAGTF G-2/S-2 all-source intelligence processing and production is essential to achieve a complete, effective, and current intelligence estimate while using the strengths and results from the other intelligence disciplines to improve SIGINT operations.

c. Interpretation

The information derived from SIGINT collection is interpreted to form logical conclusions and estimates of enemy capabilities, intentions, and future actions. This step completes the translation of the raw SIGINT information into usable intelligence.

7205. Dissemination

Dissemination is the provision of SIGINT information in a timely manner and in a usable form to commanders, other decisionmakers, or all-source intelligence analysts. Because of security requirements, dissemination of COMINT information is made primarily to SIGINT and all-source intelligence production elements such as the MAGTF AFC. Proper SIGINT C2 and supporting CIS architectures that provide accurate situational awareness, along with effective IRs and tactical requirements management, enable proper dissemination.

SIGINT dissemination planning and management involves establishing dissemination priorities, stipulating dissemination and reporting criteria, selecting dissemination means, and monitoring the flow of SIGINT reporting. The ultimate dissemination goal is to deliver SIGINT products to the appropriate user in the proper form and at the right time, while concurrently preventing the dissemination of irrelevant products and avoiding information overload.

Reporting consists of providing the SIGINT products in standardized, easily usable formats needed to satisfy tasked requirements in a timely manner. The nature of the SIGINT effort requires timely reporting to effectively exploit its intelligence value. SIGINT reports generally fall into two categories, product reports and technical reports. Standardized formats are used in the preparation and transmission of these reports for speed and compatibility. As most of these formats are classified, readers should refer to USSID 300, *SIGINT Reporting*, for specific information and examples.

a. Product Reports

Product reports are prepared by all SIGINT producers for commanders, planners, and all-source intelligence analysts. A product report contains timely, accurate, thorough, relevant, and useful SIGINT information about the adversary in response to the supported commander's PIRs and IRs. Reports may be sent periodically or may be sent whenever highly perishable data is acquired in accordance with specified intelligence reporting criteria. Generally, SIGINT product reports will fall into one of three categories:

(1) SIGINT Report. In SIGINT reports, the source of information is clearly SIGINT by the content and classification markings. Such reports generally contain the SIGINT assessment along with pertinent SIGINT technical information. These reports are handled within SCI-controlled facilities and communications channels. Within a MEF, the CE, GCE, and ACE may be included in distribution for SIGINT products. Within a MEU(SOC) or special-purpose Marine air-ground task force (SPMAGTF), the CE is generally the sole recipient of these reports. When pertinent, either these reports will be fused within all-source intelligence products for further dissemination within the MAGTF or dissemination will occur via SCI courier or briefings.

(2) Non-Codeword Report. NCW reporting procedures may be used only when authorized by DIRNSA. The principal value of NCW reporting is to allow time-sensitive dissemination of critical SIGINT information to a broader audience during high tempo operations. In NCW reports, the source of information is clearly SIGINT. However, unlike standard SIGINT product reports, the NCW report is passed directly to commanders without SIGINT markings or SI security controls to allow immediate tactical use (e.g., I&W, support to targeting, support to force protection). For example, NCW reports may be passed directly from the SSU collector to other MAGTF units (e.g., an infantry battalion) via GENSER communications (usually voice message). Typically, the format for these is the standard size, activity, location, unit, time, and equipment (SALUTE) report. Specific procedures regarding NCW reporting during operations should be contained within the SIGINT appendix to annex B of the operations order.

(3) Sanitized Report. Sanitized SIGINT reports contain SIGINT information that is reported via GENSER communications means in a manner that does not reveal SIGINT as the source of the information. The level of sanitization authority allowed the MAGTF commander is established by DOD Directive TS-5105.21-M-2, *Sensitive Compartmented Information (SCI) Security Manual, Communications Intelligence (COMINT) Policy*. Within the MAGTF, actual sanitization of SIGINT reports is generally performed by designated intelligence personnel under the guidance and supervision of the MAGTF SSO or AFC OIC. The reports are disseminated via all-source products or other GENSER intelligence reports.

b. Technical Reports

Technical reports consist of the SIGINT technical elements required by SIGINT collectors, analysts, and technical support and production agencies external to the MAGTF (e.g., call signs, frequencies, operating schedules). SIGINT technical reporting requires SCI-secure connectivity with pertinent organizations (e.g., NSA, theater RSOC, supporting CSSA) via JWICS, NSANET, or some alternate SCI communications means. Within the MAGTF, all SIGINT technical reporting is conducted by either RadBn or VMAQ's TERPES section.

7206. Utilization

SIGINT, as all intelligence, has no inherent value. Its value is realized only through its effective support of the commander's intelligence requirements or other operational requirements. Commanders, G-2/S-2s, and G-3/S-3s must continuously evaluate SIGINT operations, products, and reports for timeliness, usefulness, and overall quality and responsiveness to stated IRs. They must provide feedback to the MAGTF G-2/S-2 and SIGINT unit leaders to improve future SIGINT operations. Ultimately, SIGINT utilization provides guidance for future intelligence and SIGINT operations and management.

See appendix C, SIGINT and SCI Security Management Operations Flowchart, that summarizes the principal SIGINT planning considerations, activities, and products discussed in this chapter.

Section III. SIGINT Plans and Orders

Guidance for the conduct of SIGINT operations comes from many sources. The DIRNSA-developed USSID series are the principal SIGINT operations directives that contain policy, direction, guidance, instruction, and procedures on performing SIGINT functions in compliance with national directives and security requirements. Additionally, since MAGTFs will normally be part of a JTF or NEF, reference to joint and naval orders, guidance, and SIGINT TTPs is necessary to identify unique operating concepts and methodologies and support procedures and formats.

The MAGTF G-2/S-2 prepares SIGINT plans and orders. The intelligence operations officer coordinates the overall effort with the assistance of the SIO, other intelligence section staff officers, and the CO or OICs of organic and supporting SIGINT units. SIGINT plans and orders focus on internal MAGTF SIGINT requirements, operations, and TTP.

The SIGINT appendix will appear as appendix 2 (signals intelligence) to annex B (intelligence) in all MAGTF operations plans and orders. (See appendix D, SIGINT Appendix Format, of this manual for a recommended format for the SIGINT appendix.) It should include the following:

- Friendly forces to be utilized include—
  - Personnel augmentation requirements.
  - SIGINT units of adjacent or other theater forces and the support expected.
  - Joint force maritime component commander (JFMCC) and ATF DS SIGINT elements and CSSA available to support the landing force during amphibious operations.
  - RSOC, joint force land component commander (JFLCC), joint force air component commander (JFACC), and other component commanders or task forces capable of providing SIGINT support during JTF operations.
- Planned arrangement, employment, and use of external SIGINT support, to include any special collection, production, dissemination and CIS arrangements.
- Establishment of coordinating instructions for SIGINT operations planning and control, to include technical support expected from higher headquarters.
- MAGTF SIGINT element taskings.
- Communication and information SIGINT support.

Section IV. Execution

MAGTF SIGINT operations generally are centrally managed by the MAGTF G-2/S-2 and decentrally executed to—

ı Integrate RadBn SSU and ACE VMAQ TERPES SIGINT effectively with other MAGTF and external intelligence and reconnaissance operations.

ı Provide the most effective MAGTF intelligence requirements support.

The integration of RadBn SSU and VMAQ TERPES SIGINT collection, production, and dissemination plans and activities with those of other MAGTF and supporting intelligence organizations uses these limited resources and their mutual support more effectively (e.g., cueing). The MAGTF mission, commander's intent, threat operations and signals usage, concept of operations, and environmental considerations all influence the ultimate task organization, command relationship, concepts of employment, and tasks of SIGINT units. For example, they determine a decision to task-organize elements of the SSU in direct support of the GCE or rear area operations commanders. Such information is specified within annexes B, C, and K of the operations order or in a subsequent fragmentary order.

Figure 7-1 notionally depicts the following seven key aspects of these interrelated SIGINT operations.

ı Task organization and command or support relationships of MAGTF SIGINT units with other MAGTF elements. RadBn SSU OCAC is collocated with the MAGTF G-2/S-2 and operates in general support of the MAGTF. VMAQ and TERPES are organic and OPCON to the ACE.

ı External SIGINT units that typically support a MAGTF.

ı Principal SIGINT systems employed within and in support of the MAGTF.

ı Relationship of other MAGTF intelligence and reconnaissance units with SIGINT units.

ı Principal communications pathways, means, and level of classification.

ı Key intelligence information systems that interoperate with SIGINT systems.

ı Principal SIGINT reports disseminated via the communications pathways shown.

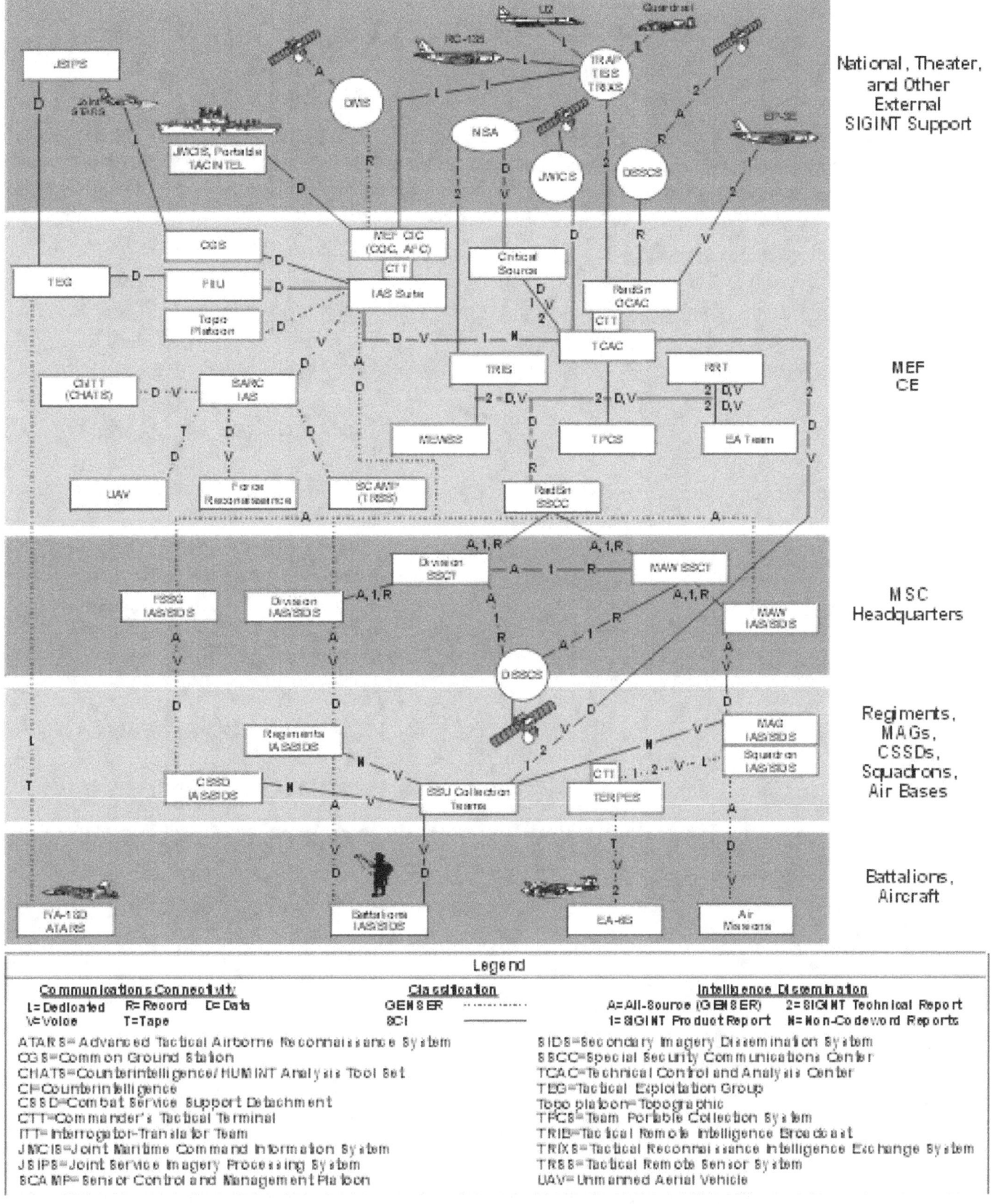

Figure 7-1. MAGTF and Supporting SIGINT Operations.

Chapter 8

Security of Sensitive Compartmented Information

SCI is classified information concerning or derived from intelligence sources, methods, or analytical processes that is required to be handled within formal access control systems established by the Director of Central Intelligence (DCI). Only intelligence and information that clearly warrant extraordinary security measures will be restricted to SCI control.

When dealing with issues involving SCI security, refer to the following publications for policy and instructions:

- Director, Central Intelligence Directive (DCID) 1/14, *Personnel Security Standards and Procedures Governing Eligibility fo Access to Sensitive Compartmented Information.*
- DCID 1/16, *Security Manual for Uniform Protection of Intelligence Processed in AISs and Networks.*
- DCID 1/21, *Physical Security Standards for Sensitive Compartmented Information Facilities.*
- Defense Intelligence Agency Manual (DI-AM) 50-4, *Department of Defense Intelligence Information Systems (DODIIS) Information Security (INFOSEC) Program.*
- Department of Defense Directive (DODD) 5105.21-M-1, *Sensitive Compartmented Information (SCI) Security Manual, Administrative Security.*
- Department of the Navy Supplement (NAVSUP) to DODD 5105.21-M-1, *SCI Administrative Security Manual.*

These documents provide policy and guidance on—

- SCI personnel and information security clearance procedures.

- SCIF and TSCIF requirements.
- Classification levels.
- Compartmentation.
- Decompartmentation.
- Sanitization.
- Release to foreign governments.
- Emergency use.
- Security policy and procedures for the protection of information controlled in SCI compartments.

Safeguarding SCI is critical. Security of SCI is important as it protects not only a piece of intelligence but also its source. For these reasons, dissemination and access to SCI information and materials are restricted. However, to be worthwhile, SCI must be accessible to commanders for use in decisionmaking. SCI must be classified only to the degree necessary in the interests of security. SCI security must be applied within the context of the mission, with security needs constantly assessed and balanced against operational mission needs.

SCI security is the responsibility of the commander, who exercises this responsibility through the unit G-2/S-2. The SSO serves as the primary staff officer for day-to-day SCI security administration and management. The commander must ensure SCI is accessed only by those persons with an appropriate clearance, access approval, identified need-to-know, and appropriate SCI indoctrination. This is accomplished by carefully managing those units and persons with SCI access and the equipment and facilities used to process, disseminate, and store SCI. (Appendix C, SIGINT and SCI Security Management Operations Flowchart, summarizes the principal SCI security planning considerations, activities, and products discussed in this chapter.)

8001. Special Security Officer

The SSO serves as the command's focal point for the receipt, control, and accountability of SCI materials and the supervision of the SCI security functions of subordinate SCIFs. The SSO will be a military commissioned officer, warrant officer, or civilian (GS-9 or above). The SSO—

- Supervises the operation of the special security office and administers the SCI security program. This includes oversight of other local SCIFs under the SSO's cognizance.

- Maintains required SCI directives, regulations, manuals, and guidelines to adequately discharge SSO duties and responsibilities.

- Ensures all SCI is properly accounted for, controlled, marked, transmitted, transported, packaged, and safeguarded. Ensures all SCI is destroyed in authorized destruction facilities and in accordance with current regulations.

- Ensures SCI is disseminated only to persons authorized access with an established need-to-know.

- Provides guidance and assistance for processing SCI access and eligibility requests.

- Serves as the official channel for passing SCI access certifications.

- Conducts or otherwise manages SCI personnel, information, physical, and technical security (i.e., TEMPEST, technical surveillance countermeasures [TSCM]) actions and procedures according to current regulations.

- Conducts SCI security briefings, indoctrinations, and debriefings; administers and maintains signed nondisclosure agreements; and performs other related personnel security actions.

- Investigates SCI security infractions, makes recommendations, prepares required reports, and initiates and supervises any necessary corrective actions.

- Conducts a continuing training and awareness program to ensure that all SCI-indoctri-

nated individuals are apprised of new requirements and guidelines.

- Ensures that appropriate accreditation documentation is available for each SCIF, TSCIF, and SCI system under the SSO's cognizance.

8002. Personnel Security Program

The protection of SCI is directly related to the effectiveness of the personnel security program. DCID 1/14 establishes the personnel security standards for the United States intelligence community. A mutually supporting series of program elements (e.g., need-to-know, investigation, binding contractual obligations on those granted access, security education and awareness, and individual responsibility) provides reasonable assurances against compromise of SCI by those authorized access to it.

a. Access Approval Authority

In accordance with DCID 1/14, the Director o Naval Intelligence is authorized to grant, deny, or revoke SCI access to Marines and Sailors. This responsibility is carried out through the Department of the Navy Central Adjudication Facility (DONCAF).

b. Requirements for SCI Access

DONCAF may grant an individual SCI access when the following requirements have been met.

(1) Need-to-Know is Determined. Even when approved for a specific access, the holder is expected to acquire or disseminate only that SCI essential to effectively carry out an assignment No person will have a need-to-know solely by virtue of rank, title, or position.

(2) Eligibility is Determined. DCID 1/14 provides eligibility standards for investigation and evaluation for an individual's access to SCI. A single-scope background investigation (SSBI) conducted within the last 5 years serves as the basis for determining access approval.

(3) SCI Billet is Identified.

DCI does not require the Navy to maintain an SCI billet structure. However, SSO Navy and CNSG have decided to retain the current SCI billet numbering system for accountability within the DON. SCI billets are administered by the local command SSO and reported annually to SSO Navy or CNSG as appropriate.

(4) Security Indoctrination is Completed

SCI indoctrination is the instruction an individual receives prior to receiving access to an SCI systems, programs, and materials. The instruction convey the unique nature, sensitivity, and special security safeguards and practices for SCI handling, particularly the necessity to protect sensitive sources and methods.

(5) Nondisclosure Agreement is Signed.

As a condition of access to SCI, individuals authorized SCI access must sign a DCI-authorized nondisclosure agreement (NDA). The NDA establishes explicit obligations on both the Government and the individual for the protection of SCI. An NDA is binding for life and cannot be revoked or waived. Failure to sign an NDA is cause for denial of SCI access.

8003. Physical Security

All SCI must be processed, used, and stored within an accredited SCIF. Accreditation is granted when the proposed facility meets the physical security standards stipulated in DCID 1/21. The SSO, DIA, is the accrediting authority for all DOD SCIFs, while NSA is the accreditation authority for all service cryptologic element SCIFs. Organizations are responsible for ensuring that SCIFs are established only when operationally re-

quired and when existing SCIFs are not adequate to support the unit's mission.

a. Sensitive Compartmented Information Facility

A SCIF is an accredited area, room, group of rooms, buildings, or installation where SCI may be stored, used, discussed, and/or electronically processed. Access to SCIFs will be controlled to preclude entry by unauthorized personnel. Non SCI-indoctrinated personnel entering a SCIF must be continuously escorted by an indoctrinated individual who is familiar with the security procedures of that SCIF. The physical security protection for a SCIF is intended to prevent as well as detect visual, acoustical, technical, and physical access by unauthorized persons.

b. Emergency Action Plans

Each accredited SCIF will establish an emergency action plan. This plan will be approved by the appropriate G-2/S-2 or SSO. The essential concern of the plan must be safety of personnel over a other factors. The plan will address—

- Physical protection of personnel working in the SCIF.
- Adequacy of fire fighting equipment and life-support equipment (e.g., oxygen and masks).
- Entrance of emergency personnel (e.g. police, medical technicians, and firemen) into a SCIF.
- Evacuation plans for persons.
- Emergency destruction and transfer procedures of classified material and equipmen in the event of—
  - Fire.
  - Loss of essential utilities.
  - Sabotage.
  - Riots.
  - Civil disorders.
  - Hostile or terrorist attack or capture.
  - Natural disasters.

c. Tactical Sensitive Compartmented Information Facility

Recognizing the need for SCIFs to support tactical operations, the DCI requires the following minimum physical security standards for a TSCIF. If the situation and time permit, these minimum standards will be improved on by using the security considerations and requirements for permanent secure facilities. (Appendix E, TSCIF Checklist, is provided as a guide when activating or deactivating a TSCIF.)

- Locate the TSCIF within the supported headquarter's defensive perimeter, preferably within its main command echelon.

- Use permanent-type facilities, if available.

- Maintain 24-hour operation under field or combat conditions.

- Establish a physical barrier around the TSCIF. Where practical, the physical barrier should be triple-strand concertina o general-purpose barbed-tape obstacle. The TSCIF approval authority determines whether proposed security measures provide adequate protection based on local threat conditions.

- Guard the TSCIF perimeter by stationing walking or fixed guards to observe the controlled area. Guards will be armed with weapons and ammunition in accordance with Marine Corps Order (MCO) 5500.6F, *Arming of Security and Law Enforcemen (LE) Personnel and the Use of Force.*

- Restrict access to the controlled area with a single gate or entrance that is guarded continuously.

- Maintain an access list. Only those people whose names appear on the list will be allowed access to the TSCIF.

- Staff the TSCIF with sufficient personnel as determined by the on-site SSO or G-2/S-2 based on the local threat conditions.

- Keep emergency destruction and evacuation plans current.

- Store SCI material in lockable containers when not in use.

- Establish and maintain communications with local security or emergency reaction forces, if possible.

- Conduct an inspection of the vacated TSCIF area. The SSO or G-2/S-2 ensures SCI materials are not inadvertently left behind when the TSCIF displaces.

- Coordinate planning with the unit's headquarters commandant, who is responsible for providing TSCIF guard personnel, communication with command post guard forces, emergency personnel reaction forces, and internal reaction forces.

d. Mobile Tactical Sensitive Compartmented Information Facility

Mobile TSCIF requirements are as follows:

- Maintain a 24-hour operation and staff the TSCIF with sufficient personnel as determined by the on-site SSO or G-2/S-2 based on the local threat conditions.

- Incorporate external physical security measures into the perimeter defense plans for the immediate area in which the mobile TSCIF is located. (A physical barrier is not required as a prerequisite to establish a mobile TSCIF.)

- Use Marines performing the day-to-day operations of the TSCIF to control external physical security.

- Establish and maintain communication with backup guard forces, if possible.

- Incorporate incendiary methods in emergency destruction plans to ensure total destruction of SCI material during emergency situations.

- Adhere to the following restrictions when using a rigid-sided shelter or portable van.

  - Mount the shelter to a vehicle so that the shelter can move on short notice.

  - Affix a General Services Administration (GSA)-approved security container permanently within the shelter. Protect the lock combination to the level of security of the material stored therein.

- Control the entrance to the mobile TSCIF with SCI-indoctrinated Marines on duty within the shelter.
- Limit entrance to the mobile TSCIF to SCI-indoctrinated personnel.
- Store classified material within the locked GSA container and secure the shelter' exterior entrance during redeployment.

- Adhere to the following restrictions when using a mobile TSCIF for a soft-sided vehicle or man-portable system.
  - Protect SCI material in an opaque container (i.e., leather pouch, metal storage box, or other suitable container that prevents unauthorized viewing).
  - Keep this container in the physical possession of an SCI-indoctrinated person.

- Limit the quantity of SCI material permitted within the mobile TSCIF to that which is absolutely essential to sustain the mission. Employ stringent security arrangements to ensure that the quantity of SCI material is not allowed to accumulate more than is absolutely necessary.

e. Tactical Sensitive Compartmented Information Facility Accreditation

The accreditation process consists of three steps, each requiring a message to be sent to the cognizant approval authority (see NAVSUP to DODD 5105.21-M-1). Approval authorities vary with respect to information and formats required. When requesting TSCIF authorization and accreditation, use the current reference from the cognizant authority. The following reports and messages are prepared by the unit SSO or G-2/S-2.

(1) Concept of Operations. A message that outlines the who, what, when, where, and why for the TSCIF and identifies supporting security, administrative, and point of contact information.

(2) TSCIF Activation Report. A report sent to the approval authority upon commencement o TSCIF operations.

(3) TSCIF Deactivation Report. A report sent to the approval authority when the TSCIF has ceased operations and has been certified to be free of SCI material.

8004. Information Systems Security

All SCIF intelligence and information systems used for processing, storing, and conveying intelligence and/or SIGINT information must be accredited prior to operating. The DON approving authority for SCIF intelligence systems is the Office of Naval Intelligence (ONI-54) in accordance with DIAM 50-4. The cognizant DON approving authority for SCIF resident cryptologic systems is CNSG (N1).

The SSO is responsible to the G-2/S-2 for overall management and administration of the unit's SCI security program and for SCIF security. The unit's information system security manager (ISSM) and the information system security officer (ISSO) complement the SSO and are accountable for the SCIF-resident information systems The ISSM or ISSO will help ensure new and changed information systems meet all security requirements. These individuals coordinate the approval of new or changed systems with the appropriate DON approving authority. Normally, the ISSM and ISSO are the principal interface between the approving authority and the local command.

Chapter 9

Training

The policies, standards, and procedures for the conduct of SIGINT training as well as the assignment of responsibilities to ensure adequate and responsive training are spelled out in DODD 5210.70, *DOD Cryptologic Training*. Additionally, MCO 1510.50A, *Individual Training Standards (ITS) System for the Signals Intelligence Ground Electronic Warfare Occupational Field (OccFld)*, provides a detailed description (by rank and MOS) of tasks SIGINT Marines must be capable of performing.

9001. Military Occupational Speciality Training

Training for the SIGINT Marine focuses on building, maintaining, and enhancing the technical skills required to be MOS proficient.

a. Entry-Level Training

The foundation for all SIGINT Marine training is the entry-level training. Due to its highly technical nature, this OccFld possesses some of the longest MOS entry-level training pipelines. The following paragraphs briefly describe these pipelines.

(1) 0206 Basic SIGINT. Following The Basic School, all SIGINT-designated lieutenants are sent to the Cryptologic Division Officers Course (CDOC), Corry Field, Pensacola, Florida. Following CDOC, all 0206 lieutenants are ordered to one of the two RadBns to develop and enhance their SIGINT skills.

(2) 7588 Electronic Warfare Officer. The initial, formal EW training for air EW lieutenants is the Joint Electronic Warfare School, Pensacola Florida. The course focuses on basic radar theory, friendly and threat integrated air defense system (IADS), naval forces organization and capabilities, and the application of EW.

Following the Joint Electronic Warfare School, 7588 lieutenants receive specialized training with the Fleet Replacement Squadron (VAQ-129), Whidbey Island, Washington. This 9-month course provides instruction and training on the EA-6B aircraft operations and systems and on threat IADS aircraft and shipping. Additionally all 7588 electronic warfare officers obtain Naval Air Training and Operating Procedures Standardization (NATOPS) program qualification in the EA-6B.

(3) 2621 Manual Morse Intercept Operator. Manual Morse training begins with Morse code training at Ft. Huachuca, Arizona. Upon graduation, the new manual Morse intercept operator reports to Corry Field, Pensacola, Florida, for the Communication Signals Collection and Processing (450) Course.

(4) 2631 ELINT Intercept Operator or Analyst. Basic ELINT training is provided by the Cryptologic Technician Course, Corry Field, Pensacola, Florida. Marines assigned to the VMAQ TERPES section also attend the TERPES Operator Course, Navy and Marine Corps Intelligence Training Center, Dam Neck, Virginia.

(5) 2651 Special Intelligence Communicator. Training in SI communications, data communications, networks, and system security is provided in the Cryptologic Technician "O" Course, Corry Field, Pensacola, Florida.

(6) 267X Cryptologic Linguist. The cryptologic linguist has the longest initial training track of any ground MOS. Training begins with basic language training at the Defense Language Institute (DLI), Monterey, California, for a period of 47 to 63 weeks, depending on the language and student's ability. Following graduation from DLI, the basic linguist will report to Goodfellow AFB, Texas, for cryptologic linguist specialist training.

(7) 2629 SIGINT Analyst. Upon completion of their initial tour, many 2621's, and some 2631's, and 267X's will attend the Fleet Analysis and Reporting Course, Goodfellow AFB, Texas, for additional training to qualify for MOS 2629, SIGINT analyst.

b. SIGINT Skill Progression Training

SIGINT Marines have a wealth of resident and nonresident training opportunities to refine, maintain, or enhance their skills. These programs are announced by HQMC and include—

- NSA Director's Fellowship Program for field grade officers.
- Junior Officer Cryptologic Career Program for company grade officers.
- Middle Enlisted Cryptologic Career Advancement Program for SNCOs.
- Military Intern SIGINT Analyst Program for SNCOs and NCOs.
- Military ELINT Signals Analyst Program for SNCOs and NCOs.
- Marine Corps Cryptologic Computer Administration Program for enlisted Marines.
- Various military linguist programs.

9002. Functional Training

Functional SIGINT training focuses on ensuring Marines in all elements of the MAGTF are aware of SIGINT contributions and the corresponding SIGINT or EW threat from our adversaries.

a. SIGINT Marines

Functional training educates SIGINT Marines on all-source intelligence operations within the MAGTF, naval forces, and JTFs. SIGINT Marines participate in exercises to learn operational intelligence requirements; the interaction between commanders and staffs and MAGTF units and intelligence sections; and the capabili-

ties, limitations, and operational support methodologies within MAGTF and other units. During exercises, SIGINT Marines interact with the G-3/S-3 and G-6/S-6 to refine coordination requirements and improve intelligence flow during actual operations.

b. SIGINT Training of Non-SIGINT Marines

Non-SIGINT Marines are trained in the capabilities and limitations of Marine, Navy, JTF, theater, and national SIGINT systems that support MAGTF operations. Equal time should be spen training these Marines on the capabilities and limitations of the adversary's SIGINT or EW systems and on individual and force protection tactics and techniques. To improve mutual understanding and eliminate misconceptions, the unique security restrictions required when dealing with SIGINT information should also be explained to and practiced by non-SIGINT Marines.

9003. Exercises

SIGINT operations in exercises are closely controlled. The same security precautions and controls are required for both the real world and exercises. USSID 56, *Exercise SIGINT*, provides guidance on obtaining and using SIGINT during exercises.

Exercise SIGINT provides commanders, staffs and units with experience in SIGINT operations, information, rules, communications, and personnel. Exercise SIGINT operations may be conducted with or without an opposition force. Care should be taken during exercises to present a realistic picture of what SIGINT systems can provide to avoid creating false expectations.

If an opposition force does not participate, exercise SIGINT may be scripted or preplanned (e.g., staff exercise [STAFFEX] or a command post exercise [CPX]). Use of scripted SIGINT in an exercise must be requested and approved by the appropriate agency well in advance of the exercise. This will allow time to script the exercise

SIGINT necessary to realistically support the scenario. Exercise planners and exercise SIGINT scripters must coordinate to ensure the SIGIN information flow is realistic. All security requirements must be maintained throughout the exercise (e.g., TSCIF activation and SCI-handling procedures).

Exercise SIGINT operations may be conducted against an opposition force (e.g., during a MAGTF field exercise). This provides more realistic training for the SIGINT element and SIGINT users. Depending on the level of the exercise, the use of simulators and national systems may be requested to add realism and enhance training These assets must be requested well in advance of the exercise and approved by the appropriate agency described in the J-TENS manual.

9004. Operational Training Objectives

The major objective for SIGINT operations training is exercising SIGINT operations in a realistic tactical environment with all elements of the MAGTF.

a. SIGINT Organizations

RadBns and VMAQs should—

- Train unit leaders, planners, and supervisory personnel to—
  - Plan and direct, process and exploit, produce, disseminate, and use unique SIGINT and integrated all-source intelligence.
  - Plan and integrate SIGINT operations with multifunctional staff operations.
  - Conduct SIGINT operations.
- Train SIGINT operators in SIGINT—
  - Operations.
  - Systems.
  - Equipment.
  - TTP.
  - Supporting operations (i.e., CIS, logistics, and intelligence).

b. G-2/S-2 and Intelligence Personnel

Intelligence personnel must be able to—

- Understand the capabilities and limitations of SIGINT collection operations and the planning, integration, coordination, and execution of SIGINT collection with multidiscipline intelligence and reconnaissance collection operations.
- Understand the capabilities and limitations of SIGINT production operations and the planning, integration, coordination, and execution of SIGINT production with all-source intelligence production operations.
- Understand the capabilities and limitations of SIGINT dissemination operations (e.g. planning, integration, coordination, and execution of routine and time-sensitive SIGINT dissemination) and the requirements, establishment, and integration of unique SIGINT and multiuse CIS architectures.

c. G-3/S-3 and Maneuver and Fires Personnel

Operations, maneuver, and fires personnel should be able to—

- Plan, coordinate, and conduct effective MAGTF SIGINT, EW, and CIS operations.
- Plan, coordinate, and conduct insertion and extraction methods.
- Site and coordinate SIGINT collection and DF teams with supporting SIGINT elements, G-2/S-2, and subordinate commanders.
- Coordinate SIGINT operations with MAGTF and subordinate units' future and current operations centers and fire support coordination centers.
- Disseminate and use SIGINT and other SCI information.

d. G-4/S-4 and Combat Service Support Personnel

Logistics and CSS personnel should understand SIGINT units' unique CSS requirements (particularly electronic maintenance and unique consumables such as batteries).

e. G-6/S-6 and Communications and Information Systems Personnel

CIS personnel must be able to plan, coordinate and integrate SIGINT CIS requirements within MAGTF and supporting CIS plans and operations.

f. Headquarters Commandant

Headquarters commandant personnel must be able to understand, plan, and provide for the SIGINT units' security requirements (particularly those associated with TSCIFs and mobile SIGINT SCIFs).

Appendix A

Radio Battalion SIGINT Support Unit Checklist

The following checklist is provided as a guide to assist the radio battalion (RadBn) SIGINT support unit (SSU) officer in charge (OIC) conduc operations. Depending on the mission, location and duration of an operation, some items may not be applicable.

Planning Stage

❏ Coordinate with the RadBn S-3 to—

○ Determine exact mission and tasking of the detachment and the authority and command relationship.

○ Review all messages related to deployment and composition of the detachment.

○ Ensure S-3 tasks companies or sections to provide required personnel to fill detachment table of organization (T/O) line numbers.

○ Request assignment of RadBn SIGINT address and producer designator digraph, if necessary.

○ Verify formats and instructions for required reports.

○ Determine if area clearances and clearance certifications are necessary and request special security officer (SSO) take appropriate action.

○ Review pertinent orders and instructions of the supported unit.

○ Identify and arrange for special training and operational requirements.

❏ Coordinate with the following supported command—

○ G-2/S-2 intelligence operations officer to determine initial intelligence collection,

production, and dissemination requirements and current intelligence estimate.

○ G-2/S-2 intelligence operations officer to determine time constraints for submission of input to appendix 2 to annex B of the operations order.

○ G-2/S-2 all-source fusion center OIC to determine plans and integration of intelligence and SIGINT production activities.

○ G-2/S-2 dissemination officer for a list of SIGINT products recipients, appropriate report formats, and routine and time-sensitive communications and information systems (CIS) plans.

○ G-2/S-2 intelligence operations officer and G-4/S-4 for supply and logistics requirements to be provided by supported command (e.g., electronic maintenance and consumables such as batteries; meals, ready to eat; maps; and fuel).

○ G-3/S-3 electronic warfare officer for electronic attack (EA) requirements and capabilities and input to appendix 3 to annex C of the operations order.

○ G-2/S-2 operations officer and G-6/S-6 to address requirements for communications support (e.g., secure and unclassified local area network [LAN] access, equipment).

○ G-3/S-3 to establish liaison teams with supported unit's subordinate elements if necessary.

○ Command security manager, G-2/S-2, and G-3/S-3 for force protection and communications security monitoring requirements and plans.

❏ Develop and publish a training schedule in coordination with the RadBn S-3 and supported unit's intelligence officer.

❏ Request courier cards from RadBn SSO for appropriate detachment personnel.

❏ Coordinate collection and analytical and production requirements with the operations control and analysis (OCA) element to—

○ Ensure the detachment analytical and production team knows the technical aspects of the operations area.

○ Ensure the analytical and production team has a current technical support package; request an update if required (i.e., hardcopy, electronic copy).

○ Ensure SIGINT position designators for equipment are current; prepare and issue required SIGINT resource status report (RSR).

○ Ensure the National Security Agency (NSA) or the pertinent regional security operations center or cryptologic shore support activity provides a current technical briefing on targets in the area of operations.

❏ Coordinate transportation requirements with RadBn S-3, S-4, and supported unit.

❏ Coordinate embarkation requirements with RadBn S-4 and supported unit to—

○ Review current embarkation orders.

○ Complete embarkation forms (e.g., Tactical Cargo Manifest Declaration, 1387-2, 1348-1).

○ Review current inbound and outbound agricultural restrictions on vehicles.

○ Assemble complete embarkation kit with guidelines for use upon departure.

○ Request table of equipment (T/E) items for detachment.

❏ Coordinate communications and information requirements with RadBn S-6 and supported unit intelligence officer and CIS officer to—

○ Determine circuit request requirement.

○ Determine telecommunications service request (TSR) requirement.

○ Determine frequency and call sign requirements and request communications-electronics operating instructions.

○ Request special intelligence (SI) routing indicator and plain language address assignments.

○ Determine communications security materials system (CMS) requirements and request that the CMS custodian have material available for issue.

○ Designate an SSO CMS custodian.

○ Determine TEMPEST inspections and automated information systems accreditation requirements.

○ Determine cryptographic hardware and keying material requirements and procedures with all communication elements.

❏ Ensure all personnel are qualified with T/O weapons and arrange for battlesight zero (BZO) firing as necessary.

Predeployment Stage

❏ Audit health records to—

○ Determine inoculations required and arrange for required shots with the corpsman.

○ Determine if detachment members or members of their families are undergoing extensive outpatient care, with an indefinite prognosis.

○ Confirm and record blood types.

○ Ensure all personnel requiring eyeglasses have two pair. Also ensure they have optical inserts for gas masks.

○ Ensure detachment members meet class I or II dental readiness.

○ Arrange for block pickup of health and dental records.

❏ Coordinate legal affairs to—

　❍ Inform personnel of advisability of wills and procedures for obtaining them.

　❍ Inform personnel of powers of attorney and procedures for obtaining them.

❏ Arrange for storage of privately owned vehicles and personal effects.

❏ Arrange for mail handling.

❏ Coordinate pay matters to—

　❍ Conduct personal financial record audit.

　❍ Prepare savings and other allotments.

❏ Coordinate administrative matters to—

　❍ Verify accuracy of record of emergency data.

　❍ Ensure identification cards are current and have proper Geneva Convention category information.

　❍ Ensure personnel have current identification (ID) tags.

　❍ Audit and update officer qualification records and enlisted service record books.

　❍ Complete change of reporting senior fitness reports, fitness report roughs, and proficiency and conduct marks.

❏ Coordinate clothing inspection and requirements to—

　❍ Ensure personnel have appropriate serviceable uniforms for all destinations.

　❍ Ensure personnel have appropriate civilian attire in accordance with local military customs of country(ies) to be visited.

　❍ Ensure temporary issue requirements draw includes the proper sizes and is coordinated through the RadBn S-4 and supported unit.

❏ Ensure baggage is appropriate and of sturdy construction.

❏ Ensure personnel know customs requirements of locations to be visited.

❏ Prepare government transportation request.

❏ Prepare military transportation authorization.

❏ Conduct the following:

　❍ Family services deployment briefing for all SSU and family members.

　❍ Red Cross brief.

　❍ Navy and Marine Corps Relief brief (to include preauthorized emergency loan applications).

　❍ Religious services brief.

　❍ Family services brief.

　❍ Key spouses brief.

❏ Assemble assigned T/E equipment required for deployment to—

　❍ Perform operational check of equipment.

　❍ Complete limited technical inspection (LTI) on all equipment.

　❍ Perform acceptance inspections on all temp-loan equipment.

　❍ Check the date of last calibration, if applicable.

❏ Arrange for draw or transfer of CMS material.

❏ Receive CMS custodial briefing from CMS custodian.

❏ Receive security requirements and emergency destruction briefing from SSO.

❏ Conduct training in accordance with established detachment training schedule.

❏ Coordinate with the RadBn SSO and classified materials control officer to—

　❍ Designate a detachment classified material secondary control point and custodian.

❍ Ensure required single-scope background investigation periodic reviews are initiated on those detachment personnel identified as needing updates.

❍ Request sensitive compartmented information (SCI) clearance certification on all detachment personnel be forwarded to cognizant units and other organizations as necessary.

❑ Coordinate with the RadBn adjutant or S-1 to—

❍ Draw record books.

❍ Pick up orders.

❍ Establish report criteria.

❍ Arrange for administrative and legal briefs.

❍ Arrange for detachment Uniform Code of Military Justice and code of conduct briefings.

❑ Coordinate with RadBn SSO to—

❍ Confirm security requirements.

❍ Pick up courier cards for specified personnel.

❍ Receive area intelligence briefs to include customs, politics, religion, and standards of personal conduct.

❍ Receive counterintelligence area threat briefs.

❍ Ensure all required personnel receive appropriate special access indoctrination(s).

❍ Transfer necessary technical material from SSO and OCA classified material control center accounts.

❑ Coordinate with RadBn S-3 to—

❍ Establish SIGINT operations report criteria.

❍ Determine topographic and map requirements and request allowance from OCA or the supported unit.

❍ Request preparation of appropriate cryptologic technical kits from NSA or the supporting cryptologic shore support activity.

❑ Coordinate with RadBn S-4 supply to establish fiscal account job order numbers and sign the consolidated memorandum receipt.

❑ Coordinate with RadBn S-4 electronic maintenance to—

❍ Establish equipment maintenance procedures.

❍ Establish electronic maintenance support and prepare pre-expend bin support block.

❍ Ensure that all equipment receives a predeployment LTI.

❍ Ensure skeleton record jackets are prepared for all equipment.

❑ Coordinate with RadBn S-4 motor transport and engineer to—

❍ Establish equipment maintenance procedures.

❍ Establish motor transport and engineer support.

❍ Ensure skeleton record jackets are prepared for all vehicles.

❑ Coordinate with RadBn S-4 ordnance officer to—

❍ Determine weapon requirements and other ordnance needs.

❍ Obtain proper storage boxes for the transport of weapons.

❍ Draw weapons.

❍ Conduct necessary inspections.

❍ Conduct daily sight counts.

❍ Determine ammunition and pyrotechnic training requirements during deployment.

❏ Coordinate with RadBn S-4 embarkation officer to—

   ❍ Receive embarkation package.

   ❍ Determine dunnage requirements.

❏ Draw equipment and sign for gear assigned to detachment.

❏ Receive medical brief from battalion medical personnel.

❏ Contact special services officer for recreation items.

❏ Publish the final—

   ❍ Detachment T/O and T/E.

   ❍ Roster of personnel.

   ❍ Dependent point-of-contact roster.

   ❍ Equipment and uniforms required.

   ❍ Detachment training schedule.

   ❍ Detachment operations order.

❏ Palletize or combat load supplies and equipment.

❏ Coordinate embarkation of personnel and equipment with S-4 of supported unit.

❏ Stage for embarkation.

Deployment

❏ Coordinate with G-2/3 and S-2/3 for initial location of combat operations center, combat intelligence center, and collection direction finding (DF) and EA teams.

❏ Continue coordination of collection and DF team and radio reconnaissance team locations with G-2/S-2 collections officer and G-3/S-3. Include updates for inserts, extract times, and methods.

❏ Coordinate with G-2/S-2 intelligence operations officer for inputs and presentation for intelligence estimate, concept of operations, and intelligence operations plans briefings.

❏ Submit the following required reports and messages:

   ❍ Activation report and deactivation report to RadBn S-3 and supported unit G-2/S-2.

   ❍ Circuit activation report to RadBn S-6 and supported unit G-6/S-6.

   ❍ Administrative reports to RadBn S-1.

   ❍ CMS destruction reports to SSO or CMS.

   ❍ Circuit deactivation report to RadBn S-6 and supported unit G-6/S-6.

   ❍ Transportation request to RadBn and supported unit G-4/S-4.

   ❍ Required analysis and technical reports to OCA and supported unit G-2/S-2. (RSR to NSA upon activation and deactivation.)

   ❍ Tactical SCI facility activation and deactivation reports to Commander, Naval Security Group, supported unit SSO, and others as appropriate.

❏ Prepare and distribute required reports to the supported commander.

❏ Send deactivation message.

Postdeployment

❏ Turn in weapons and classified material immediately upon return.

❏ Participate in supported unit operations debriefings as required. Debrief with RadBn commanding officer and S-3 on the first working day after return.

❏ Coordinate with RadBn adjutant, S-1, S-3, and S-4 to—

   ❍ Return record books to S-1.

   ❍ Return medical and dental records.

❍ Terminate temporary additional duty (TAD) orders.

❍ Prepare and submit performance evaluation reports and proficiency and conduct marks as required for the TAD period.

❍ Notify mail clerk to stop forwarding mail.

❍ Return technical material to the OCA platoon.

❑ Return CMS material to CMS custodian within 48 hours of return.

❑ Return courier cards to SSO.

❑ Prepare equipment for postdeployment LTI.

❑ Ensure proper maintenance is conducted on equipment prior to returning to respective companies or sections.

❑ Turn in equipment on equipment repair orders and note any equipment damage or problems.

❑ Settle fiscal account.

❑ Submit an after action report within 20 days of return (or as directed) to the supported unit G-2/S-2, G-3/S-3, and RadBn S-3.

❑ Disband detachment.

❑ Prepare award recommendations on deserving personnel.

❑ Recommend necessary changes to unit SOPs and coordinate with the RadBn and supported unit staff.

Appendix B

Marine Corps SIGINT Equipment

Radio battalions (RadBns) and Marine tactical electronic warfare squadrons (VMAQs) use unique specialized equipment for the search, detection, identification, processing and exploitation of enemy signals of interest (SOIs), and the subsequent production and dissemination of SIGINT products. The following sections describe the primary SIGINT equipment in the inventory of the RadBns and VMAQs.

Section I. Radio Battalion SIGINT Equipment

AN/ULQ-19(V)2 Electronic Attack Set

The AN/ULQ-19(V)2 electronic attack (EA) set (figure B-1) provides the capability to conduct spot or sweep jamming of single-channel, encrypted or unencrypted, voice or data signals operating in the standard military frequency range of 20-79.975 MHz from selected mobile platforms (e.g., high mobility, multipurpose wheeled vehicles [HMMWVs], mobile electronic warfare support system [MEWSS], helicopters). In addition, it can provide up to four channels of high-power VHF voice and/or data communications when not being used as a jamming system. When employed as a tactical, general-purpose, low-VHF jamming system, it has a 250-watt radio frequency linear amplifier that produces a nominal 200 watts of effective radiated power (ERP) using a standard omnidirectional whip antenna. To provide required jamming, the system must be employed and operated from a location with an unobstructed signal line of sight to the target enemy's communications transceiver.

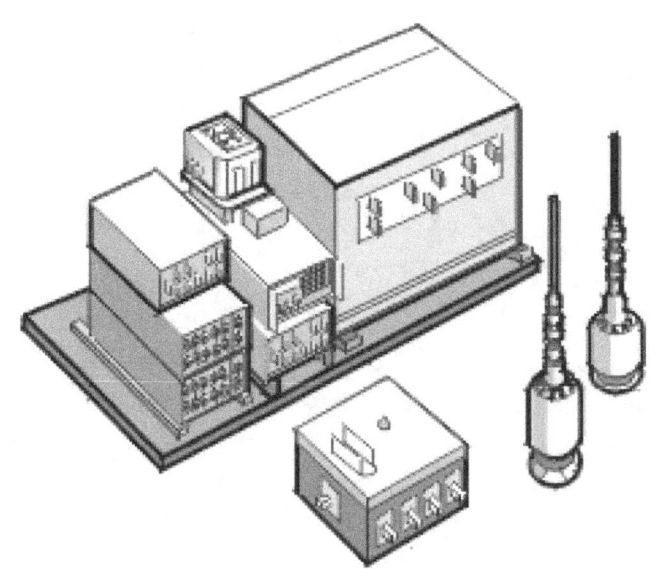

Figure B-1. AN/ULQ-19(V)2.

AN/MLQ-36 Mobile Electronic Warfare Support System

The AN/MLQ-36 MEWSS provides a multifunctional capability that gives SIGINT electronic warfare (EW) operators limited armor protection (figure B-2). This equipment is ideally suited to provide SIGINT EW support for highly mobile mechanized and military operations in urban terrain where maneuver and/or armor protection is critical. MEWSS comprises a signals intercept system, a radio direction finding (DF) system, an EA system, a secure communications system, and an intercom system installed in a logistics variant of the light armored vehicle (LAV)-25. Electronic warfare support (ES) activities are accomplished through the use of two WJ-8618B(S1) acquisition receivers and the WJ-32850 MANTIS DF system. EA activities are conducted with the AN/ULQ-l9(V) electronic attack set.

Figure B-2. AN/MLQ-36.

AN/MLQ-36A Mobile Electronic Warfare Support System Product Improvement Program

The mobile electronic warfare support system product improvement program (MEWSS-PIP) is an advanced SIGINT/EW system integrated into an LAV (figure B-3). The MEWSS-PIP provides a total replacement of the EW mission equipment now fielded in the AN/MLQ-36 MEWSS. It provides the ground commander with a mobile SIGINT/EW system capable of operating in a variety of tactical situations. The primary mission of the MEWSS-PIP is to provide intercept, collection, automated DF, and EA against threat modern communications and noncommunications emitters across a broad frequency range. It is a multiservice, open-systems architecture developed by the Marine Corps and the Army that incorporates elements of the Army's intelligence and electronic warfare common sensor (IEWCS) system. This system enhances interoperability through cooperative engagement, data sharing, and precision location. Initial operational capability is scheduled for fourth quarter, fiscal year 1999.

Figure B-3. AN/MLQ-36A.

AN/PRD-12 Direction Finder Set

The AN/PRD-12 is a tactical, man-transportable system that provides search, intercept, and DF on communications signals in the HF/VHF/UHF bands (figure B-4). Up to four PRD-12 stations can be networked, providing DF data to a mission control station via radio link with single-channel ground and airborne radio system (SINCGARS) equipment. Each station has the ability to function as the net control station. When stations are net-worked, they provide target emitter position data to mission control via voice link. A complete station can be relocated rapidly, optimizing its use in forward areas with combat units.

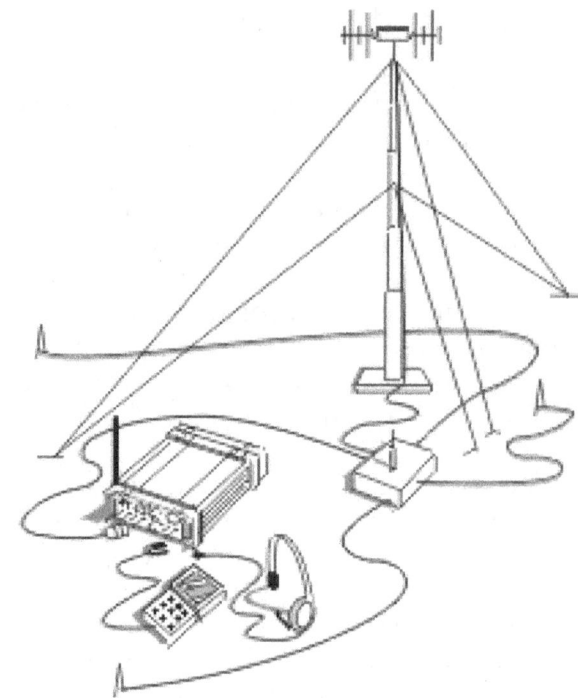

Figure B-4. AN/PRD-12.

AN/MSC-63A Communications Central

The AN/MSC-63A is a shelterized communications switch that provides a secure semiautomated data communications switch and terminals for the processing of general service (GENSER) or defense special security communications system (DSSCS) sensitive compartmented information (SCI) record message traffic. See figure B-5. There is one AN/MSC-63A with each Marine division and Marine aircraft wing special security communications team, and three AN/MSC-63A's with each RadBn. The system consists of three functional subsystems: shelter and auxiliary support subsystem, the communications subsystem, and the data processing subsystem. See figure B-6. The AN/MSC-63A is fully compatible with the Army's AN/TYC-39.

Figure B-5. AN/MSC-63A.

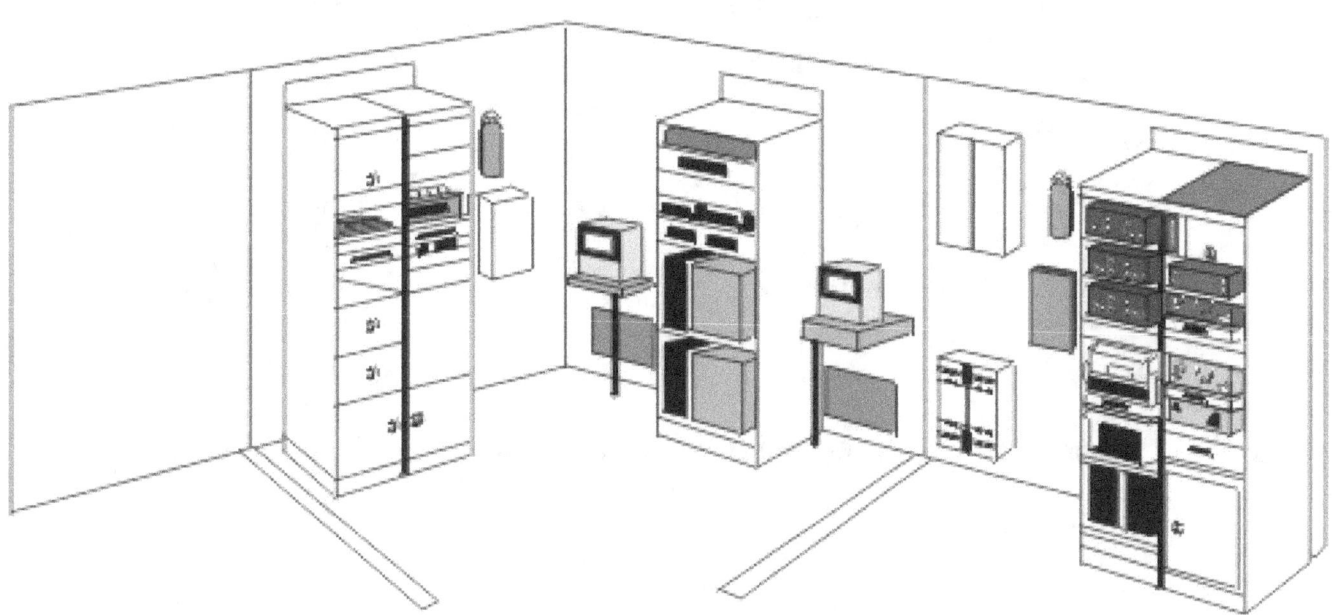

Figure B-6. AN/MSC-63A (interior view).

AN/TSQ-130(V)2/(V)5 Technical Control and Analysis Center

The AN/TSQ-130(V)2/(V)5 technical control and analysis center (TCAC) is an all-weather, tactical, transportable, SIGINT-processing, analysis and reporting system installed in a large, self-contained, modified S-280G shelter. TCAC is the primary system used by the RadBn SIGINT support unit. It is capable of performing semiautomated-SIGINT collection management, data base maintenance, analysis, technical and tactical reporting, and SIGINT technical control of forward deployed RadBn elements or teams. The (V)2 is the baseline system, while the (V)5 has upgraded communications capabilities. See figure B-7 for a notional TCAC concept of employment.

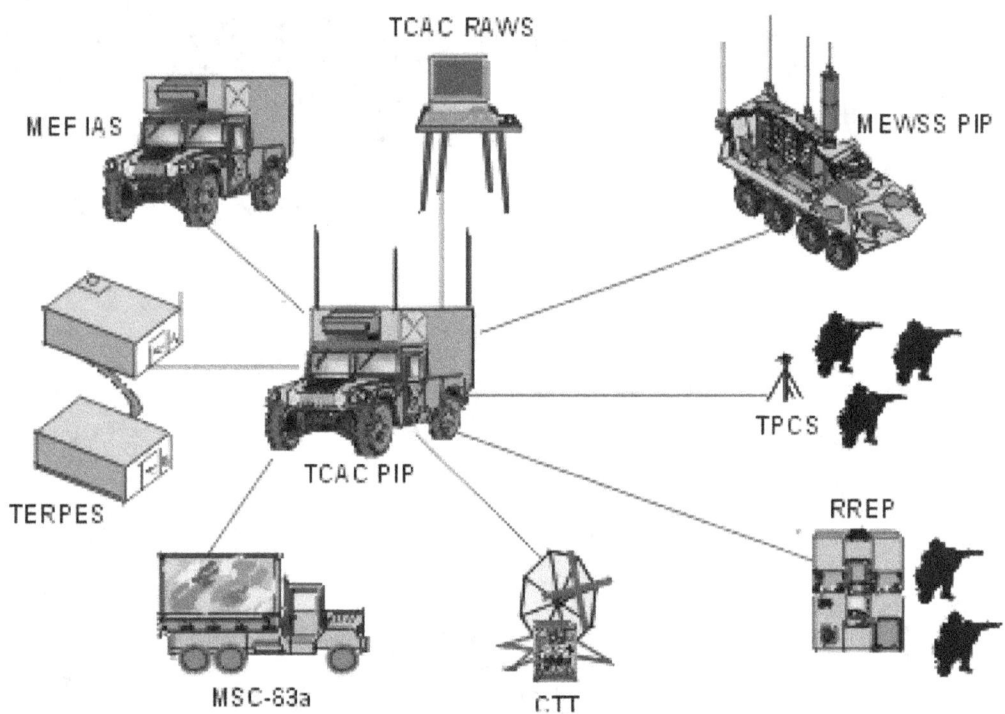

Figure B-7. Technical Control and Analysis Center Concept of Employment.

AN/MYQ-8 TCAC-PIP

The AN/MYQ-8 TCAC-PIP will replace the TCAC. It will consist of three remoteable analysis workstations (RAWSs), one communications interface module (CIM), and one supervisor control module (SCM). Each workstation will consist of modularly designed component equipment fully integrated to perform their intended functions.

Remoteable Analysis Workstation

RAWS provides the capability to perform necessary analysis and reporting functions at a central location or a more forward deployed site, remoted from the TCAC shelter. During shelter operations, a RAWS will be electrically interconnected to the other terminals in the shelter. During remote operations, a RAWS will be connected to the shelter via local area network (LAN) or radio link. It could operate in a stand-alone mode.

Communications Interface Module

CIM provides man-machine interface to communication subroutines that support the interface between the TCAC PIP and other RadBn systems (e.g., team portable collection system, mobile electronic warfare support system) or external intelligence agencies.

Supervisor Control Module

SCM provides a man-machine interface to file server and supervisor subroutines to support system control and overall supervision of the TCAC PIP workstations.

AN/USC-55 Commander's Tactical Terminal

The AN/USC-55 commander's tactical terminal (CTT) is a multiservice-developed, special application, UHF satellite communications receiver that can be dedicated to receive critical, time-sensitive intelligence by commanders and intelligence centers at all echelons, in near-real-time, at GENSER or SCI levels. The receiver provides one full-duplex and two receive-only channels. Planned concept of employment for CTT is similar to that of the tactical receive equipment (TRE) fielded widely within the MAGTF to allow access to intelligence broadcasts and intelligence collectors and producers. Full operational capability for CTT is expected during fiscal year 1999.

Team Portable Collection System Upgrade

The team portable collection system (TPCS) upgrade (figure B-8) is a semiautomated, man-transportable communications intelligence (COMINT) system. It provides intercept, collection, radio direction finding, analysis, reporting, and collection management support. The system provides significant SIGINT capabilities in a modular configuration that can be deployed by component as a stand-alone COMINT system or as part of the integrated RadBn SIGINT and MAGTF intelligence efforts. TPCS uses state-of-the-art equipment that consolidates information and expedites the delivery of critical COMINT to MAGTF and external commanders and agencies. The upgrade will extend the frequency range of the system and provide capabilities against modern signals.

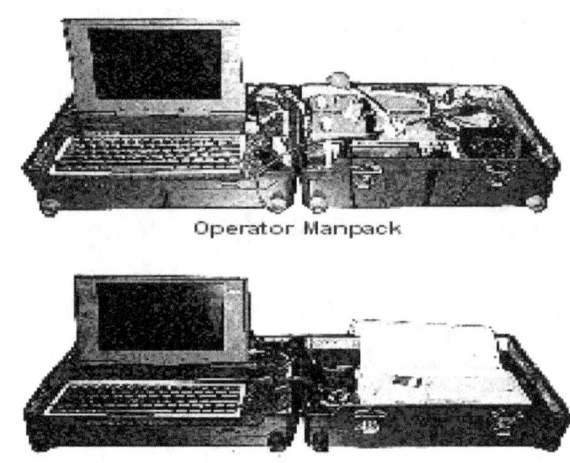

Figure B-8. Team Portable Collection System Upgrade.

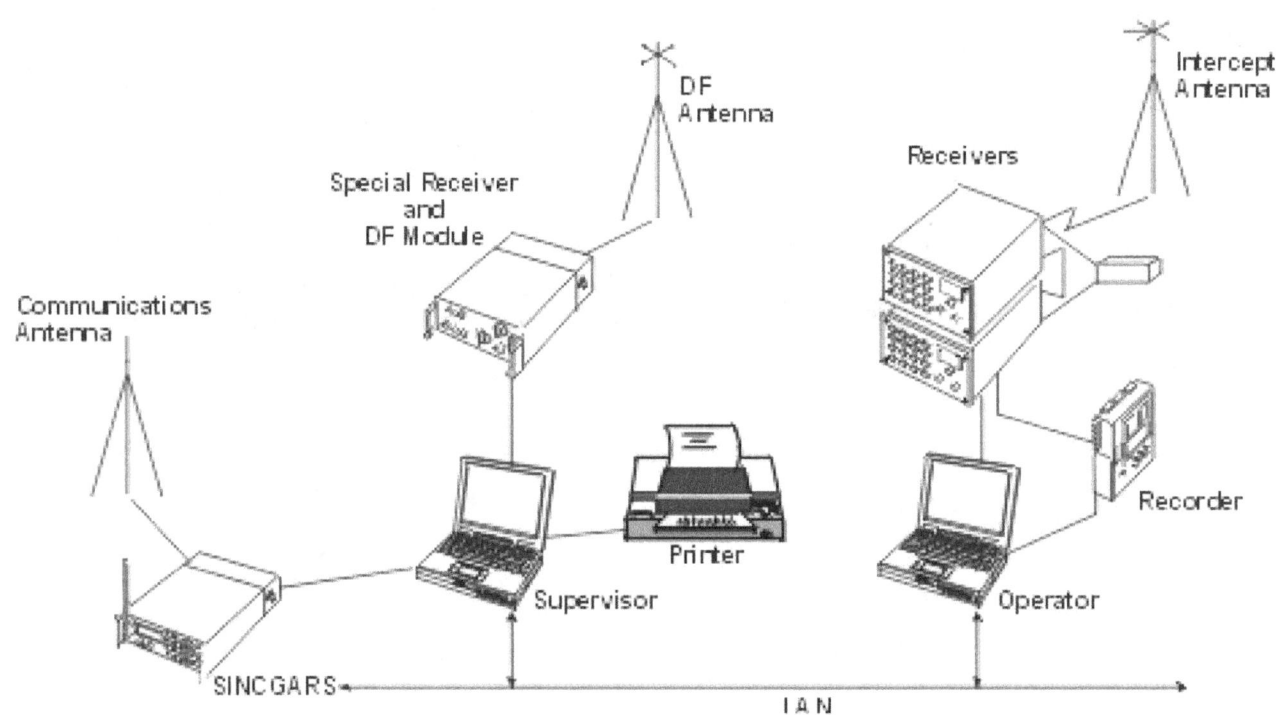

Figure B-9. Team Portable Collection System COMINT Collection Subsystem.

TPCS upgrade is comprised of three subsystems: a COMINT collection subsystem (CCS), including the AN/PRD-12 direction finding set (to be replace by TOPMAKER) and collection receivers (see figure B-9 on the facing page); an analysis subsystem (AS) (figure B-10); and a communications subsystem (CS). Modern single-channel radio nets are used to link TPCS upgrade outstations with the RadBn TCAC to allow automated processing and dissemination of collected information and ultimate dissemination to the MAGTF G-2/S-2 and other organizations. Full operational capability for TPCS upgrade is expected by the second quarter of fiscal year 2001.

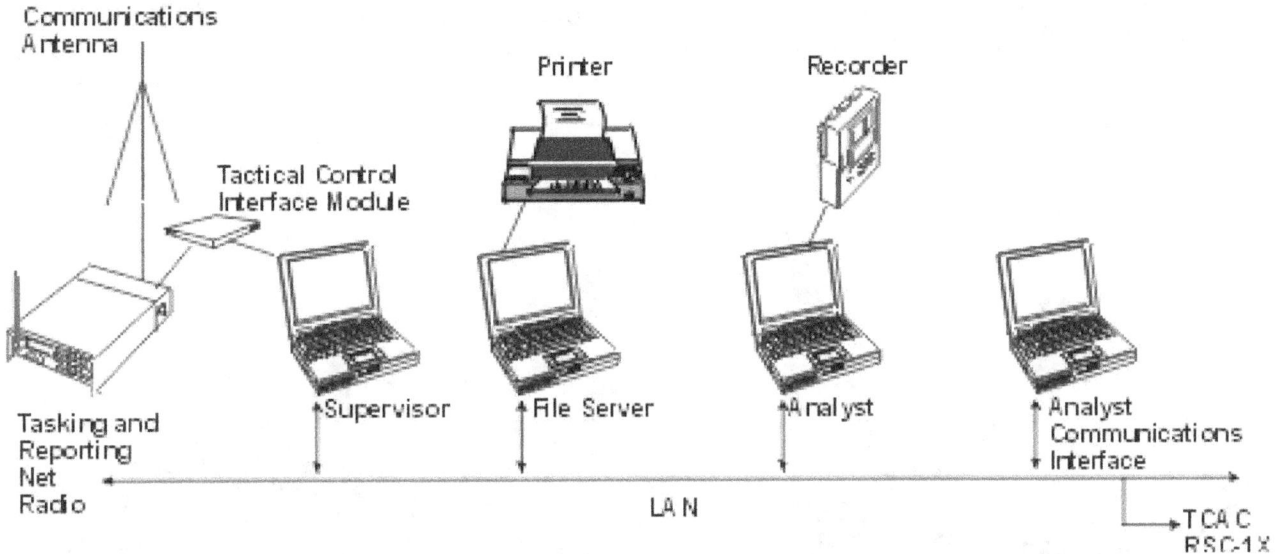

Figure B-10. Team Portable Collection System Analysis Subsystem.

Trojan Spirit II

Trojan Spirit II (TS II) is a mobile SHF satellite communications (SATCOM) system that uses commercial or military satellites to receive, transmit, and process secure, voice, data, video teleconferencing (VTC), and facsimile communications. See figure B-11. TS II provides 14 channels of digital voice or data (SCI or GENSER) with a maximum aggregate data rate of 1.544 megabytes per second (Mbps). LAN communications are supported by SCI and GENSER ethernets.

Routers provide access to the secret internet protocol router network, the Joint Worldwide Intelligence Communications System, National Security Agency platform, and the defense SATCOM system. These capabilities provide the necessary dedicated communications for coordinating MAGTF SIGINT and other intelligence operations. The system consists of three HMMWVs with mounted standard integrated command post lightweight multipurpose shelters, tunnel-mounted power generation units, a towed 2.4 meter (C, Ku-band), and a 6.1 meter (C, Ku, X-band) antenna.

Figure B-11. Trojan Spirit II.

Radio Reconnaissance Equipment Program

The radio reconnaissance equipment program (RREP) SIGINT suite (SS)-1 is a semiautomated, integrated radio intercept and DF system composed of a ruggedized computer and six functional modules that plug together. See figure B-12. RREP SS-1 modules may operate independently or semi-independently through the use of the ruggedized, handheld computer system. It is designed to enable preplanned product improvements and future technology upgrades. The selected equipment will enable the radio reconnaissance teams (RRTs) to target the majority of low-level, single-channel, unencrypted tactical signals of interest used by military, police, insurgents, and other potential hostile forces throughout the world. RREP SS-1 will be employed by RRTs during advance force, preassault and deep postassault conventional, and special operations, under any environmental, climatic, or weather conditions. The system is designed to lighten the individual RRT Marine's combat load as well as to enhance the RRT's operational signal search and technical data base development collection operations.

The RREP SS-2 will provide a highly deployable, man-transportable, signals intercept and DF system employed by RRTs in support of the entire spectrum of MAGTF operations. See figure B-13. RREP SS-2 employs advanced receiver capabilities, cellular phone and other digital communications collection and DF technology, global positioning system map navigation software, a more modular design, and electronic attack capabilities. As with RREP SS-1, the SS-2 operates at the modular level and at the integrated system level. The system can be controlled manually or via subcompact personal computer.

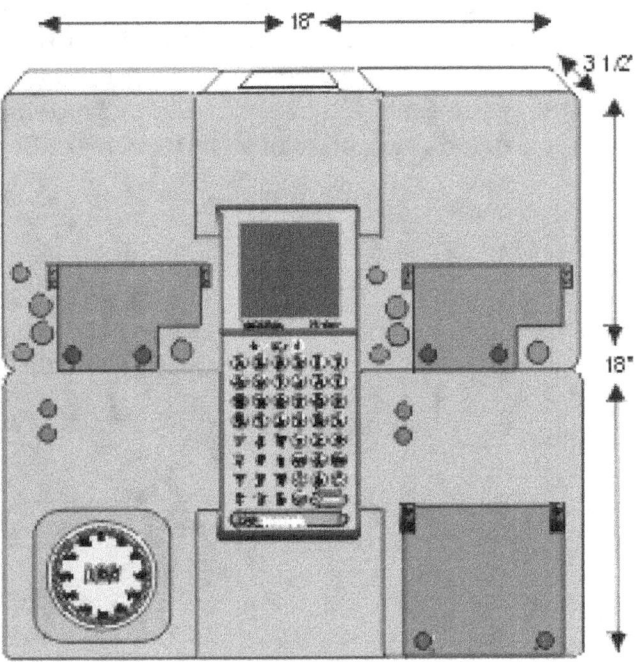

Figure B-12. RREP SS-1.

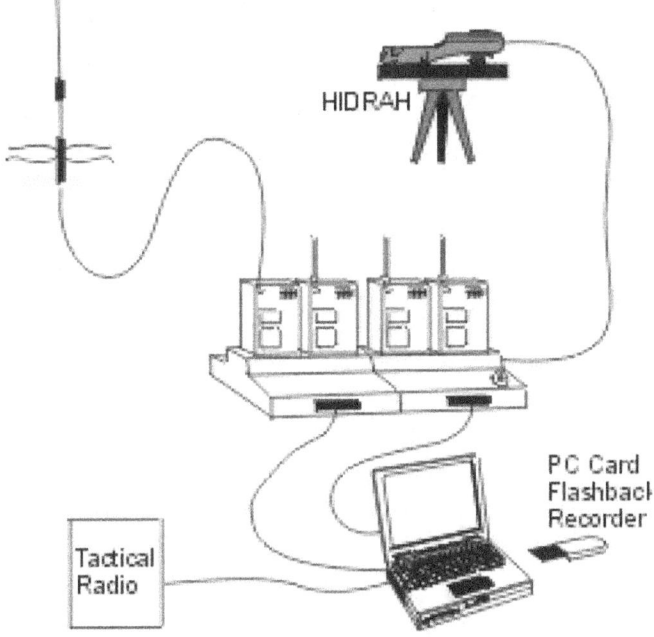

Figure B-13. RREP SS-2.

The handheld integrated directional receiver and homing (HIDRAH) system is a man-transportable, tactical, cordless, radio intercept and signal line-of-bearing (LOB) DF system consisting of several commercial off-the-shelf items of equipment fully integrated in a single, ruggedized and weather-resistant housing. HIDRAH provides RRTs with a threat I&W capability during radio reconnaissance foot-mobile patrols and signal homing support for tactical recovery of aircraft and personnel operations. The HIDRAH system has a unique design that may be employed independently in a handheld manner or by mounting it to an M16 rifle (figure B-14).

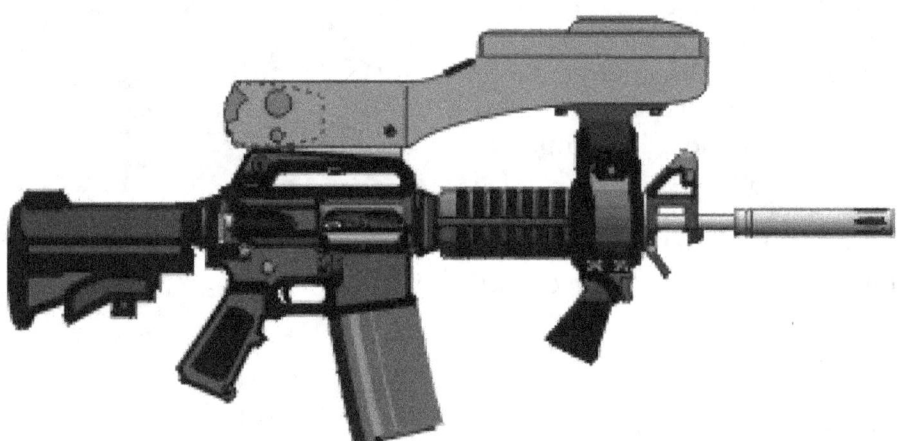

Figure B-14. Rifle-Mounted HIDRAH.

Section II. Radio Battalion SIGINT Equipment Technical Characteristics

Designator	Description	Frequency Coverage	Modulation
AN/MLQ-36	MEWSS; COMINT collect/process/analysis; EA	20-80 MHz (collection and DF expandable to 500 MHz)	AM, FM, ICW, SSB, FSK
AN/MLQ-36A	MEWSS-PIP; COMINT/ELINT collect/process/geolocation; EA	0.5 MHz - 40 GHz	conventional, low probability of intercept
AN/PRD-12	direction finder set, man packable	.5 - 500 MHz	AM, FM, ICW, SSB, FSK
AN/ULQ-19(V)2	electronic attack set; EA	20 - 79.975 MHz	FM
AR-2002	commercial VHF/UHF frequency scanner; COMINT	25 - 550 MHz, 800 - 1300 MHz	AM, FM
AR-2500	commercial HF/VHF/ UHF frequency scanner; COMINT	1 - 1500 MHz	AM, FM, CW, SSB
AR-2515	commercial HF/VHF/ UHF frequency scanner; COMINT	5 - 1500 MHz	AM, FM
AR-3000	commercial HF/VHF/ UHF frequency scanner; COMINT	0.1 - 2036 MHz	AM, FM, CW, SSB
EB-100	receiver, miniport VHF/UHF; DF	20 - 1000 MHz intercept and DF	AM or FM
HEXJAMS	hand-emplaced, expendable jammers	barrage jam 20 - 80 MHz	NA
HIDRAH	COMINT collection, DF	.1 - 1900 MHz intercept 25 - 1000 MHz DF	AM, FM, USB, LSB, CW
IC-R71A	general coverage HF receiver; COMINT	0.1 - 30 MHz	AM, FM, CW
IC-R7000	general coverage VHF/UHF receiver; COMINT	25 - 1300 MHz	AM, FM, SSB
IC-R9000	general coverage HF/VHF/UHF receiver; COMINT	0.1 - 1999.80 MHz	AM, FM, CW, SSB
ICF-PR080	commercial HF/VHF handheld frequency scanner; COMINT	.15 - 108 MHz & 115.15 - 223 MHz	AM, FM, SSB
MPR-88	receiver, miniport VHF/UHF, ruggedized; COMINT	20 - 1000 MHz intercept	AM or FM
R-2174(P)/URR	radio receiver, general purpose, HF; COMINT	0.5 - 29.999 MHz	AM, FM, CW, SSB
RREP SS-1	COMINT collection, DF	1 - 2000 MHz intercept 25 - 1000 MHz DF	AM, FM, USB, LSB, CW
RREP SS-2	COMINT collection, DF	.1 - 1900 MHz intercept 25 - 1000 MHz DF	AM, FM, USB, LSB, CW
WJ-8616	radio receiver, general purpose, HF; COMINT	0.5 - 29.999 MHz	AM, FM, CW, SSB
WJ-8618	radio receiver, general purpose, VHF/UHF; COMINT	20 - 500 MHz	AM, FM, CW, pulse
WJ-8654	radio receiver, general purpose, COMINT	.5 MHz - 1.0 GHz	AM, FM, CW, pulse

Section III. VMAQ SIGINT and EW Equipment

EA-6B Prowler

The EA-6B Prowler (figure B-15) is a subsonic advanced warfare carrier capable aircraft, powered by twin turbojet engines. The crew is composed of one pilot and three electronic countermeasure officers. The AN/ALQ-99 tactical jamming system effectively incorporates receivers and external pods for power and transmission of jamming signals. The Prowler receives and processes designated signals of interest (SOIs) for jamming selected SOIs for subsequent processing and analysis and employs the AGM-88 high-speed antiradiation missile (HARM).

Figure B-15. EA-6B Prowler.

AN/TSQ-90D/E(V) TERPES

The AN/TSQ-90D/E(V) tactical electronic reconnaissance processing and evaluation system (TERPES) receives, processes, evaluates, and displays electronic reconnaissance and EA mission information received from the EA-6B aircraft and other theater and national electronic intelligence (ELINT) assets (figure B-16). TERPES also assists the MAGTF aviation combat element's (ACE) air strike mission planning and intelligence requirements. It is a multisource, integrated, tactical ELINT data processing, correlation, and fusion system installed in a S-280-size transportable shelter. TERPES supports the ELINT and EA/ES mission and VMAQ and MAGTF ACE commander's intelligence requirements. TERPES may be transported by aircraft, shock-mounted air-ride commercial or tactical ground vehicle, or attachable mobilizer for short distances.

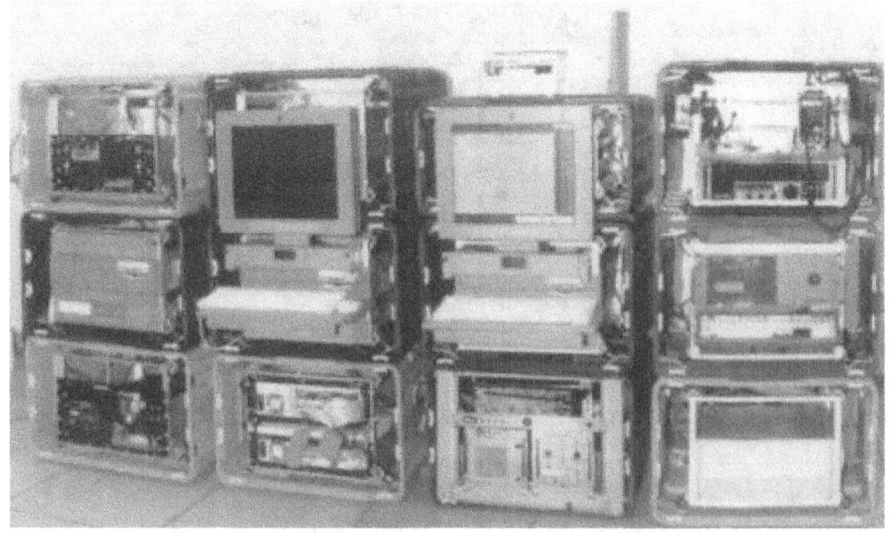

Figure B-16. AN/TSQ-90D/E(V), TERPES Portable Unit.

Appendix C

SIGINT and SCI Security Management Operations Flowchart

The flowchart on the following pages summarizes the principal SIGINT and SCI security planning considerations, activities, and products discussed in this publication.

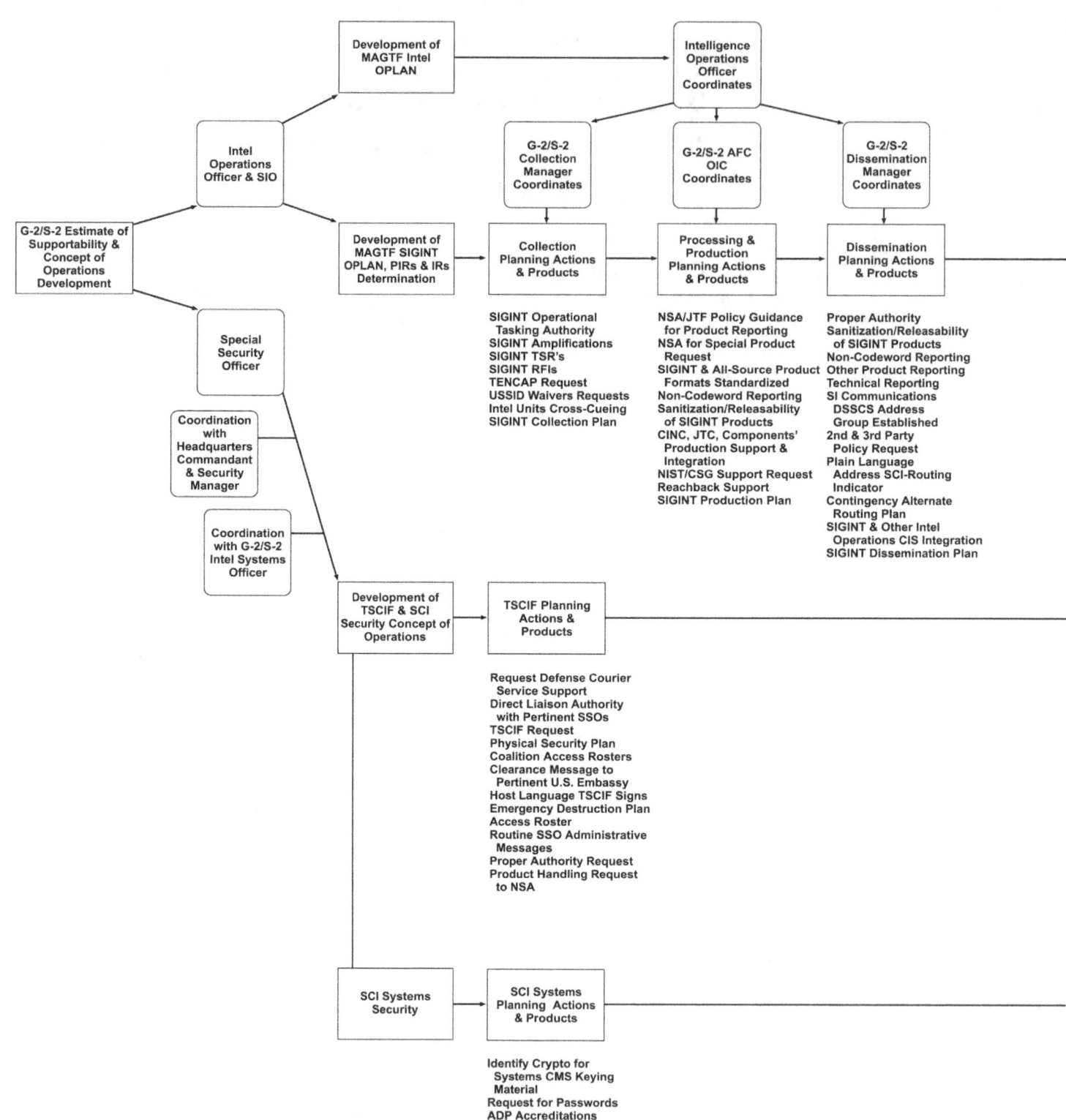

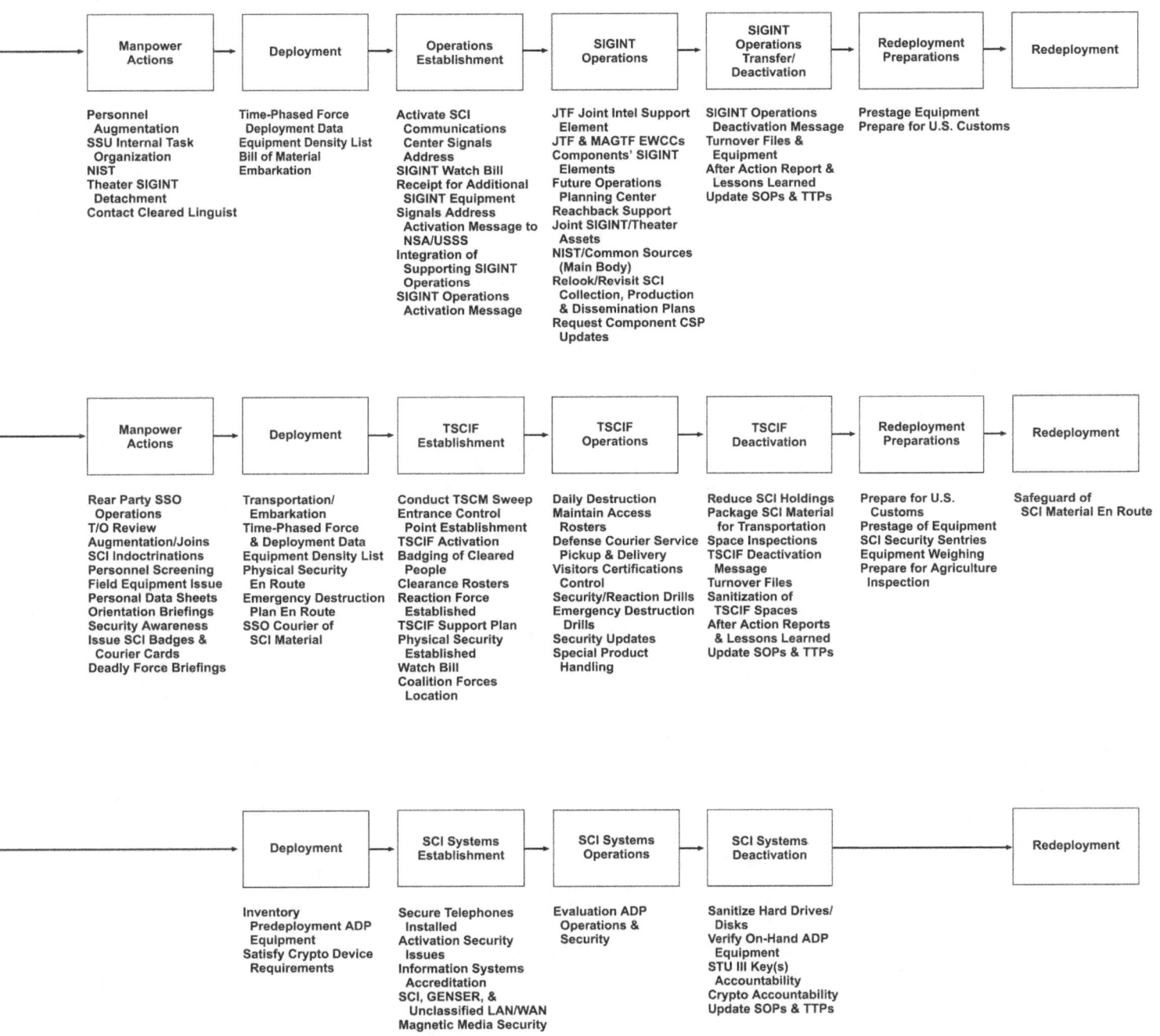

Manpower Actions

Personnel
  Augmentation
SSU Internal Task
  Organization
NIST
Theater SIGINT
  Detachment
Contact Cleared Linguist

Deployment

Time-Phased Force
  Deployment Data
Equipment Density List
Bill of Material
Embarkation

Operations Establishment

Activate SCI
  Communications
  Center Signals
  Address
SIGINT Watch Bill
Receipt for Additional
  SIGINT Equipment
Signals Address
  Activation Message to
  NSA/USSS
Integration of
  Supporting SIGINT
  Operations
SIGINT Operations
  Activation Message

SIGINT Operations

JTF Joint Intel Support
  Element
JTF & MAGTF EWCCs
Components' SIGINT
  Elements
Future Operations
  Planning Center
Reachback Support
Joint SIGINT/Theater
  Assets
NIST/Common Sources
  (Main Body)
Relook/Revisit SCI
  Collection, Production
  & Dissemination Plans
Request Component CSP
  Updates

SIGINT Operations Transfer/ Deactivation

SIGINT Operations
  Deactivation Message
Turnover Files &
  Equipment
After Action Report &
  Lessons Learned
Update SOPs & TTPs

Redeployment Preparations

Prestage Equipment
Prepare for U.S. Customs

Redeployment

Manpower Actions

Rear Party SSO
  Operations
T/O Review
Augmentation/Joins
SCI Indoctrinations
Personnel Screening
Field Equipment Issue
Personal Data Sheets
Orientation Briefings
Security Awareness
Issue SCI Badges &
  Courier Cards
Deadly Force Briefings

Deployment

Transportation/
  Embarkation
Time-Phased Force
  & Deployment Data
Equipment Density List
Physical Security
  En Route
Emergency Destruction
  Plan En Route
SSO Courier of
  SCI Material

TSCIF Establishment

Conduct TSCM Sweep
Entrance Control
  Point Establishment
TSCIF Activation
Badging of Cleared
  People
Clearance Rosters
Reaction Force
  Established
TSCIF Support Plan
Physical Security
  Established
Watch Bill
Coalition Forces
  Location

TSCIF Operations

Daily Destruction
Maintain Access
  Rosters
Defense Courier Service
  Pickup & Delivery
Visitors Certifications
  Control
Security/Reaction Drills
Emergency Destruction
  Drills
Security Updates
Special Product
  Handling

TSCIF Deactivation

Reduce SCI Holdings
Package SCI Material
  for Transportation
Space Inspections
TSCIF Deactivation
  Message
Turnover Files
Sanitization of
  TSCIF Spaces
After Action Reports
  & Lessons Learned
Update SOPs & TTPs

Redeployment Preparations

Prepare for U.S.
  Customs
Prestage of Equipment
SCI Security Sentries
Equipment Weighing
Prepare for Agriculture
  Inspection

Redeployment

Safeguard of
  SCI Material En Route

Deployment

Inventory
  Predeployment ADP
  Equipment
Satisfy Crypto Device
  Requirements

SCI Systems Establishment

Secure Telephones
  Installed
Activation Security
  Issues
Information Systems
  Accreditation
SCI, GENSER, &
  Unclassified LAN/WAN
Magnetic Media Security

SCI Systems Operations

Evaluation ADP
  Operations &
  Security

SCI Systems Deactivation

Sanitize Hard Drives/
  Disks
Verify On-Hand ADP
  Equipment
STU III Key(s)
  Accountability
Crypto Accountability
Update SOPs & TTPs

Redeployment

(reverse blank)

Appendix D

SIGINT Appendix Format

This appendix should explain how SIGINT elements supporting or under the operational control of the MAGTF will be used to support this plan. It should also provide guidance to subordinate commanders for the conduct of SIGINT operations and the support of SIGINT elements and personnel identified to fulfill the SIGINT requirements in this plan.

CLASSIFICATION

Copy no.___ of ___ copies
Issuing Unit
PLACE OF ISSUE
Date/time group
Message reference number

APPENDIX 2 (Signals Intelligence) to ANNEX B (Intelligence) to Operation Order _____ ( )

Ref: (a) Unit standing operating procedures (SOPs) for intelligence and counterintelligence

  (b) Combatant commander, joint task force, or other higher authorities' operation orders (OPORDs) and tactics, techniques, and procedures directives

  (c) (List other documents that provide guidance required for SIGINT and supporting operations planning functions.)

1. ( ) SITUATION

  a. ( ) Enemy Situation. (Reference Appendix 8 [Intelligence Estimate] to Annex B. Describe the threat and potential threat, the basic situation and the SIGINT operations perspective. Identify the enemy's command and contro tactical and electronic orders of battle; and estimates of the enemy's centers of gravity, critical vulnerabilities, intentions, capabilities, and possible courses of action pertinent to SIGINT operations. When possible, identify finished intelligence products supporting these findings. Reference Annex B and current intelligence estimates for threat capabilities, limitations, vulnerabilities, order o battle, and assessed courses of action.)

(Page number)

CLASSIFICATION

CLASSIFICATION

b. ( ) <u>Friendly Situation</u>. (Reference Annex C [Operations] and other pertinent sources.)

c. ( ) <u>SIGINT Support Available</u>. (Reference Annex A [Task Organization], Annex B, and other pertinent sources. Identify organic, attached, and supporting SIGINT elements available to support MAGTF intelligence operations. Specify elements attached to or in direct support of any subordinate unit.)

2. ( ) <u>MISSION</u>

(State concisely the SIGINT mission as it relates to the command's planned operation.)

3. ( ) <u>EXECUTION</u>

a. ( ) <u>Concept of Operations</u>. (Summarize pertinent command relationships, task organization, main and supporting efforts, and the scope of MAGTF and supporting SIGINT and relevant all-source intelligence operations.)

b. ( ) <u>Tasks for SIGINT and Subordinate Units and Task Force Commanders and Officers in Charge (OICs)</u>.

(1) ( ) Radio battalion (RadBn) SIGINT support unit (SSU) commanding officer or OIC

(2) ( ) Aviation combat element commander (special attention to VMAQ tasks)

(3) ( ) Ground combat element (GCE) commander

(4) ( ) Rear area operations center (RAOC) commander

(5) ( ) (Others as appropriate)

(This section may include direction, requirements, authority, and other guidance regarding SIGINT elements placed in direct support of MAGTF subordinate element. Also it may include tactical sensitive compartmented [SCI] facilities, special security offices, physical security, and personnel supporting SIGINT and SCI operations, etc.)

(Page number)

CLASSIFICATION

CLASSIFICATION

c.　( )　<u>Coordinating Instructions</u>. (Restatement of MAGTF priority intelligence requirements; detailed procedures for intelligence requirements management; SIGINT support requests; direct liaison among subordinate commanders, MAGTF SIGINT units, staff officers, and pertinent external organizations and agencies; routine and time-sensitive reporting and formats; etc.)

4.　( )　<u>ADMINISTRATION AND LOGISTICS</u>

a.　( ) <u>Logistics</u>. (Reference Annex D [Logistics]. Identify unique combat service support requirements, procedures, and guidance to support MAGTF SIGINT units and operations. Specify procedures for specialized technical logistics support necessary from external organizations [e.g., from Director, National Security Agency, or via service cryptologic element channels].)

b.　( )　<u>Personnel</u>. (Reference Annex E [Personnel]. Identify SIGINT-unique personnel requirements and concerns, including global sourcing support and contracted linguist requirements.)

c.　( )　<u>Consolidated Listing and Impact Assessment of Shortfalls and Limiting Factors</u>. (Provide a consolidated listing and impact assessment of personnel and equipment shortfalls and other limiting factors that significantly affect unit SIGINT operations and support. Identify resource problems and specify key tasks that might not be accomplished adequately.)

5.　( )　<u>COMMAND AND CONTROL</u>

(Reference the MAGTF's and SIGINT units' SOPs and Appendix 10 [Intelligence Operations Plan]. Provide guidance as appropriate on the following, including internal unit and external organizations' command and control [C2])

a.　( )　<u>Command Relationships</u>. (Reference Annex J [Command Relationships]. Provide any instructions necessary regarding command relationships arrangements that will influence MAGTF SIGINT operations, with special attention to C2 relationship concerning SIGINT elements attached to or in direct support of MAGTF subordinate units.)

b.　( )　<u>Information Management</u>. (Reference Annex U [Information Management], Annex C [Operations], and Appendix 10 to Annex B. Provide any instructions necessary regarding information management [e.g., time-sensitive and routine SIGINT reporting criteria, SIGINT data bases, administration and access, reports] that will influence MAGTF SIGINT operations.)

(Page number)

CLASSIFICATION

CLASSIFICATION

c.   ( ) <u>Communications and Information Systems (CIS)</u> . (Reference Appendix 10 to Annex B and Annex K [Communications and Information Systems]. Provide any instructions necessary regarding CIS that will influence MAGTF SIGINT operations.)

d.   ( ) <u>SIGINT C2 Nodes and Facilities.</u> (Reference the MAGTF's and SIGINT units' SOPs and Appendix 10 to Annex B. Provide any guidance and instructions necessary regarding the establishment and operations of SIGIN C2 nodes and facilities [e.g., the operations control and analysis center, amphibious task force ship's signals exploitation spaces] and their integration with other MAGTF C2 nodes [e.g., the MAGTF all-source fusion center, the surveillance and reconnaissance center, the reconnaissance operations center, the amphibious task force intelligence center, electronic warfare coordination center].)

/s/ _____

_____

OFFICIAL

/s/ _____

_____

TABS:

A - Communications Intelligence Operations Requirements

B - Electronic Intelligence Operations Requirements

C - (Others as appropriate: routine and time-sensitive reporting formats, SIGINT CIS plan, etc.)

CLASSIFICATION

CLASSIFICATION

Copy no.___ of ___ copies
Issuing Unit
PLACE OF ISSUE
Date/time group
Message reference number

TAB A (Communications Intelligence Operations Requirements) to APPENDIX 2 (Signals Intelligence) to ANNEX B (Intelligence) to Operation Order _____ ( )

1.   ( )   <u>GENERAL</u>

(The purpose of this tab is to identify operations requirements for communications intelligence [COMINT] support to the planned MAGTF operation.)

NOTE: SCI controls may require this tab to be published separately from the basic OPORD, Annex B and/or Appendix 2.

 a.   ( )   (Orient COMINT collection, processing and exploitation, production, and dissemination efforts to answer the questions listed in paragraphs 2 and 3 below.)

 b.   ( )   (These requirements should address both organic and external direct support SIGINT resources tasked to support the MAGTF.)

 c.   ( )   (Reference other pertinent portions of Annex B and current intelligence estimates.)

2.   ( )   <u>COMINT OPERATIONS REQUIREMENTS AND MANAGEMENT</u>

 a.   ( )   <u>Classification</u>. (Designate the overall classification of the information included. Assign the lowest classification possible consistent with established security guidelines.)

 b.   ( )   <u>Statement of Requirement</u>. (Describe in detail COMINT information need, priority, specification of timeliness, location accuracy, and periodicity using the following format:

  (1)   ( )   <u>Requirement</u>. A detailed narrative statement of the requirement.

(Page number)

CLASSIFICATION

CLASSIFICATION

    (2) ( ) <u>Priority</u>. The priority of each requirement specification, using the following criteria for assigning priority:

      (a) ( ) <u>Priority 1</u>. Intelligence vital to successful plan implementation (forms the basis for the most crucial operational decisions).

      (b) ( ) <u>Priority 2</u>. Intelligence of critical importance to plan implementation, required for making operational decisions and planning future operations.

      (c) ( ) <u>Priority 3</u>. Intelligence of major importance to plan implementation, including intelligence required for the security of significant numbers of United States (and allied) forces.

      (d) ( ) <u>Priority 4</u>. Intelligence of considerable importance to plan implementation (makes important contribution to operational decisionmaking and planning).

      (e) ( ) <u>Priority 5</u>. Intelligence of moderate importance to plan implementation (makes moderate contribution to operational decisionmaking and planning).

      (f) ( ) <u>Priority 6</u>. Intelligence of some importance to plan implementation (contributes in a measurable way to operational decisionmaking and planning).

      (g) ( ) <u>Priority 7</u>. Intelligence of interest to plan implementation.

    (3) ( ) <u>Time</u>. (Identify the maximum delay acceptable for receipt of information by the intended user [e.g., within 10 minutes after recognition].)

    (4) ( ) <u>Location Accuracy</u>. (Identify the minimum locational accuracy for which the information is needed [e.g., 95-percent confidence, within 1 kilometer of center mass, within 25 kilometers of emitter location].)

    (5) ( ) <u>Periodicity</u>. (Identify the maximum amount of time that should pass before the target is covered again [i.e., once every 24 hours or once every 8 hours].)

(Page number)

CLASSIFICATION

CLASSIFICATION

    c.   ( ) <u>User Echelon(s)</u>. (Identify the primary echelon needing the information [e.g., GCE, RAOC]. List multiple users only if all data elements o subparagraph 2c above are the same for all listed echelons; otherwise, restate the requirement.)

    d.   ( ) <u>Geographic Area</u>. (Specify the geographic area for which the requirement specification applies, defined precisely [i.e., Country X, 0 to 50 km from western border; or Country Y, 50 to 75 km from southeastern border].)

    e.   ( ) <u>Justification</u>. (For each requirement specification, indicate the operational function(s) or purpose(s) [i.e., artillery targeting or air reconnaissance planning].)

3.   ( ) <u>UPON IMPLEMENTATION OF THE OPORD</u>. (List, in the manner described above, the COMINT operational requirements that become relevant upon implementation of the plan. Use subsequent paragraphs to reflect additional support requirements for planned phases of combat operations.)

(Page number)

Appendix E

TSCIF Checklist

The following checklist is provided as a guide when activating and deactivating a tactical sensitive compartmented information facility (TSCIF). The security measures identified should be improved upon as the situation permits. Refer to Director of Central Intelligence Directive (DCID) 1/21, *Physical Security Standards for Sensitive Compartmented Information Facilities*, and Department of Defense Directive (DODD) 5105.21-M-1, *Sensitive Compartmented Information (SCI) Security Manual, Administrative Security*, for detailed TSCIF operations policy and procedures.

TSCIF Activation

❑ Obtain site location from advance party personnel.

❑ Submit request to establish TSCIF to cognizant special security officer (SSO).

❑ Assign vehicle and/or shelter locations to site personnel.

❑ Move vehicles into site position. Ensure SCI containers remain locked and guarded unt site is accredited.

❑ Configure site for operation needs and ease of future movement.

❑ Erect shelters, antennas, and camouflage.

❑ Establish internal communications (SSO to access control point and emergency reaction force).

❑ Review and implement guard procedures.

❑ Emplace barrier material and restriction signs.

❑ Establish a 24-hour, single-gate access point (shelter with lights). Provide guards with access roster of authorized personnel.

❑ Determine location of destruction site (burn barrel, etc.).

❑ Conduct briefings (i.e., operations security, emergency destruction, emergency evacuation, shift schedule, reaction force, perimeter defense, badge system).

❑ Doublecheck physical security of site.

❑ Accredit site; declare site secure.

❑ Inventory SCI documents and materials as they are unpacked.

❑ Inform G-2/S-2 of commencement of TSCIF operations.

❑ Begin SCI operations and communications.

❑ Send TSCIF activation message.

TSCIF Deactivation

❑ Receive the order to terminate operations.

❑ Coordinate deactivation time with the G-2/S-2.

❑ Zeroize communications security (COMSEC) equipment; ensure message queues are emptied.

❑ Establish guards for SCI materials; inventory and pack SCI into locked containers.

❑ Debrief all one-time access personnel.

❑ Ensure all magnetic media is degaussed a minimum of three times each and all teletype, printers, and/or typewriter ribbons are destroyed or secured with SCI material.

❑ Sweep all SCI work areas for SCI and other classified materials, including telephone directories, newspapers, magazines, notepads, trash bags, etc. Check desk drawers, underneath desks and boxes, equipment containers, bulletin boards, acetate overlays, etc.

❑ Ensure all SCI is either packed in proper containers for redeployment or destroyed using established procedures.

❑ Account for all TSCIF badges and access rosters.

❑ Make a final inspection of the TSCIF and declare it officially deactivated.

❑ Send TSCIF deactivation message.

❑ Ensure all personnel are briefed on movement time and location and SCI is properly controlled.

❑ Upon termination of operations, return to garrison SCIF, reinventory and account fo all SCI material, reset all combination locks, clear all hand receipts, and clean equipment.

❑ Update standing operating procedure and files with lessons learned during the operation.

Appendix F

Glossary

Section I

Acronyms and Abbreviations

AAW .... antiair warfare
ACE .... aviation combat element
ADCON .... administrative control
ADP .... automatic data processing
AFB .... Air Force base
AFC .... all-source fusion center
AI .... area of interest
AIA .... Air Force Intelligence Agency
AIG .... addressee indicator group
AM .... amplitude modulation
AMP .... amplifier
AO .... area of operations
AS .... analysis subsystem
ATARS .... advanced tactical airborne
reconnaissance system
ATF .... amphibious task force
ATFIC .... amphibious task force
intelligence center
ATO .... air tasking order
AWACS .... airborne warning and
control system

BDA .... battle damage assessment
BE .... basic encyclopedia
Bn Hq .... battalion headquarters
bps .... bits per second
BZO .... battlesight zero

C2 .... command and control
C2W .... command and control warfare
C4I .... command, control, communications,
computers, and intelligence
Capt .... captain
CATF .... commander, amphibious task force
CCE .... company command element
CCIR .... commander's critical information
requirements
CCS .... COMINT collection subsystem
CDOC .... cryptologic division officers course

Cdr .... commander
CE .... command element
CGS .... common ground station
CHATS .... counterintelligence/HUMINT
analysis tool set
CI .... counterintelligence
CIC .... combat intelligence center
CIM .... communications interface module
CINC .... commander in chief
CIS ...... communications and information systems
CJTF .... commander, joint task force
CLF .... commander, landing force
CLT .... company liaison team
CMC .... Commandant of the Marine Corps
CMO .... collections management officer
CMS .... COMSEC materials system
CNSG .... Commander, Naval Security Group
CO .... commanding officer
COC .... current operations center
COMINT .... communications intelligence
comm .... communications
COMMARFOR .... commander, Marine Corps
forces
COMMARFORLANT .... Commander,
Marine Corps Forces,
Atlantic
COMMARFORPAC .... Commander,
Marine Corps Forces,
Pacific
COMSEC .... communications security
CONPLAN .... contingency plan
Cpl .... corporal
CPX .... command post exercise
CRITICOMM .... critical communications
CS .... communications subsystem
CSG .... cryptologic support group
CSP .... cryptologic support plan
CSS .... combat service support
CSSA .... cryptologic shore support activity

CSSD .... combat service support detachment
CSSE .... combat service support element
CTT .... commander's tactical terminal
CW ....continuous wave

DASC............................ direct air support center
DCI .... Director of Central Intelligence
DCID.. Director of Central
Intelligence Directive
DCS............................ Defense Courier Service
DF ....direction finding
DIA .... Defense Intelligence Agency
DIAM......... Defense Intelligence Agency manual
DIRNSA...................... Director, National Security
Agency
DLI ....Defense Language Institute
DMS.............................Defense Message System
DOD .... Department of Defense
DODD............... Department of Defense directive
DON ....Department of the Navy
DONCAF .... Department of the Navy Central
Adjudication Facility
DS .... direct support
DSSCS ....defense special security
communications system

EA .... electronic attack
EA-6B ....all weather electronic attack
....aircraft (Prowler)
ECAC.................... Electromagnetic Compatibility
Analysis Center
ECMO............ electronic countermeasures officer
ECU ....environmental control unit
e.g.. for example
EHF .... extremely high frequency
ELINT ....electronics intelligence
EM ....electromagnetic
EMCON ....emission control
EOB .... electronic order of battle
EP ....electronic protection
EPL ....ELINT parameters list
ERP ....effective radiated power
ES ....electronic warfare support
EW ....electronic warfare
EWCC .... electronic warfare coordination
center
EWDS .... electronic warfare data base
system
EWIR ....electronic warfare integrated
reprogramming

EWMSNSUM.......... EW mission summary report
EWO ....electronic warfare officer

FDM .... frequency division multiplexing
FIE .... fly-in echelon
FIIU.................force imagery interpretation unit
FISINT .... foreign instrumentation signals
intelligence
FM .... frequency modulation
FMF ....Fleet Marine Force
FMFM .... Fleet Marine Force manual
FSCC................... fire support coordination center
FSK ....frequency shift key
FSSG..........................force service support group

G-1 .... manpower or personnel staff officer
G-2 .... intelligence staff officer
G-3 .... operations staff officer
G-4 .... logistics staff officer
G-6 .... communications and information
systems officer
GCE ....ground combat element
GENSER .... general service
GHz...gigahertz
GS .... general support; general schedule
GSA .... General Services Administration
GySgt .... gunnery sergeant

H&S ....headquarters and service
HARM .... high-speed antiradiation missile
HF .... high frequency
HIDRAH...............handheld integrated directional
receiver and homing
HMMWV...................high mobility, multipurpose
wheeled vehicle
HQMC .... Headquarters, Marine Corps
HUMINT .... human resources intelligence

I&W .... indications and warning
IAA ....Intelligence Analysis Application
IADS .... integrated air defense system
IAS ....intelligence analysis system
ICR.................intelligence collection requirement
ICW.......................... interrupted continuous wave
ID .... identification
IDR.......... intelligence dissemination requirement
i.e...that is
IEWCS .... intelligence and electronic
warfare common sensor
IMINT ....imagery intelligence

INSCOM .... U.S. Army Intelligence and Security Command
intel .... intelligence
IPR .... intelligence production requirement
IR ....intelligence requirement
ISSM .... information system security manager
ISSO .... information system security officer
ITS ....individual training standards
ITT .... interrogator-translator team

JC2WC .... Joint Command and Control Warfare Center
JCS .... Joint Chiefs of Staff
JDISS ....joint deployable intelligence support system
JFACC ...... joint force air component commander
JFC ....joint force commander
JFLCC....................... joint force land component commander
JFMCC................joint force maritime component commander
JIC ....joint intelligence center
JISE..................joint intelligence support element
JMCIS ....joint maritime command information system
JSC..................................joint spectrum center
JSIPS .... Joint Service Imagery Processing System
J-TENS........................ Joint Tactical Exploitation of National Systems
JTF ....joint task force
JWICS..................... Joint Worldwide Intelligence Communications System

LAN ....local area network
LAV .... light armored vehicle
LCpl ....lance corporal
LE...law enforcement
LOB .... line of bearing
LOS .... line of sight
LSB .... lower sideband
Lt...lieutenant
LTI .... limited technical inspection

MAG ....Marine aircraft group
MAGTF .... Marine air-ground task force
MARDIV .... Marine division
MARFOR ....Marine Corps forces
MarSptBn .... Marine support battalion

MASINT .... measurement and signature intelligence
MATCD ..... Marine air traffic control detachment
MAW ....Marine aircraft wing
Mbps .... megabytes per second
MCB.. Marine Corps base
MCO .... Marine Corps Order
MCW ....modulated continuous wave
MCWP ......Marine Corps warfighting publication
MECDL .... mission equipment control data link
MEF ....Marine expeditionary force
MEU ....Marine expeditionary unit
MEU(SOC) ....Marine expeditionary unit (special operations capable)
MEWSS ....mobile electronic warfare support system
MEWSS PIP ....mobile electronic warfare support system product improvement program
MHz ....megahertz
MIDB .... modernized integrated data base
MISSI.................... multilevel information system security initiative
MOS .... military occupational specialty
MSC ....major subordinate command
MSE ....major subordinate element
MSgt..master sergeant
MSPF .... maritime special purpose force
MUX .... multichannel radio

NATO .... North Atlantic Treaty Organization
NATOPS .... Naval Air Training and Operating Procedures Standardization
NAVSUP .... Navy supplement
NCA .... National Command Authorities
NCO ....noncommissioned officer
NCOIC .... noncommissioned officer in charge
NCS...net control station
NCW .... non-codeword
NDA............................nondisclosure agreement
NEF ....naval expeditionary force
NID ....naval intelligence data base
NIMA.................. National Imagery and Mapping Agency
NIPRNET........ nonsecure internet protocol router network
NIST................ national intelligence support team
NMCC......... National Military Command Center

NRO .... National Reconnaissance Office
NRT .... near-real-time
NSA .... National Security Agency
NSANET .... National Security Agency Network
NSG .... Naval Security Group
NSGA.................. Naval Security Group Activity
NSOC.......... National Security Operations Center
NTF....................................... naval task force
NTTC .... Naval Technological Training Center

OAS .... offensive air support
OBREP................................ order of battle report
OCA .... operations control and analysis
OCAC ...... operations control and analysis center
OccFld ....occupational field
OIC.. officer in charge
OLT..............................OCAC liaison team
ONI ....Office of Naval Intelligence
OOB ....order of battle
OPCON .... operational control
OPLAN ....operation plan
OPNAV ....Office of the Chief of
Naval Operations
OPORD ....operation order
OTH .... over the horizon
OWO ....operations watch officer

PCM .... pulse code modulation
PIP .... product improvement program
PIR ....priority intelligence requirement
PU .... participating unit

RadBn .... radio battalion
RAOC .... rear area operations center
RAWS............... remoteable analysis workstation
recon.. reconnaissance
RF.. radio frequency
RFI ....request for intelligence
RREP .... radio reconnaissance equipment
program
RRP....................... radio reconnaissance platoon
RRT .... radio reconnaissance team
RSOC............ regional security operations center
RSR .... resource status report
RU ....reporting unit

S-1 .... manpower or personnel staff officer
S-2 ....intelligence staff officer
S-3 ....operations staff officer
S-4 ....logistics staff officer

S-6.. communications
and information systems staff officer
SALUTE .... size, activity, location, unit,
time, and equipment
SARC .... surveillance and reconnaissance
center
SATCOM ....satellite communications
SCAMP.............. sensor control and management
platoon
SCE .... service cryptologic element
SCI ....sensitive compartmented information
SCIF ....sensitive compartmented
information facility
SCM ....supervisor control module
SCR .... single-channel radio
Sgt .... sergeant
SHF ....super high frequency
SI ....special intelligence
SIDS.................secondary imagery dissemination
system
SIGINT ....signals intelligence
SINCGARS .... single-channel ground and
airborne radio system
SIO .... signals intelligence officer
SIPRNET .... secret internet protocol router
network
SNCO.....................staff noncommissioned officer
SNCOIC .... staff noncommissioned
officer in charge
SOC ....special operations capable
SOI..signal of interest
SOP ....standing operating procedure
SOTA .... SIGINT operational tasking authority
SPINTCOMM ....special intelligence
communications
SPMAGTF .... special-purpose Marine
air-ground task force
SS ....SIGINT suite
SSB ....single sideband
SSBI .... single-scope background investigation
SSCC .... special security communications
center
SSCT ....special security communications team
SSE.................................SIGINT support element
SSES .... ship's signals exploitation space
SSgt... staff sergeant
SSO .... special security officer
SSOC .... special security operations center
SST......................................SIGINT support team
SSU .... SIGINT support unit

STAFFEX .... staff exercise
STU III .... secure telephone unit-type III

TACC......... tactical air command center (USMC)
tactical air control center (USN)
TACELINT .... tactical ELINT
TACINTEL .... tactical intelligence
TACREP .... tactical report
TACSAT.......................................tactical satellite
TAD .... temporary additional duty
TADIL ....tactical digital information links
TAMPS .... Tactical Aircraft Mission
Planning System
TAOC .... tactical air operations center
TCAC .... technical control and analysis center
TCAE .... technical control and analysis element
TCIM ....tactical control interface module
TCO ....tactical combat operations
TDDS ....tactical receive equipment and related
applications program data
dissemination system
TDN .... tactical data network
T/E ....table of equipment
TEAMS .... tactical EA-6B mission
planning system
TECHCON.................................technical control
TEG..............................tactical exploitation group
TENCAP ....tactical exploitation of national
capabilities program
TEPP ....TERPES ELINT preprocessor
TERPES ....Tactical Electronic Reconnaissance
Processing and Evaluation System
TFP..............................TERPES fusion processor
TIBS...........tactical information broadcast system
TJS ....tactical jamming system

T/O .... table of organization
topo .... topographic
TPCS ....team portable collection system
TPFDD..............................time-phased force and
deployment data
TPU ....TERPES portable unit
TRAP ....TRE and Related Applications
TRE ....tactical receive equipment
TRIB ....tactical remote intelligence broadcast
TRIXS .... Tactical Reconnaissance Intelligence
Exchange System
TRSS........................tactical remote sensor system
TS II .... Trojan Spirit II
TSCIF................ tactical sensitive compartmented
information facility
TSCM ..... technical surveillance countermeasures
TSR ....telecommunications service request
TTP ....tactics, techniques, and procedures

UAV................................unmanned aerial vehicle
UHF .... ultra high frequency
USAF ....United States Air Force
USB .... upper sideband
USMC ....United States Marine Corps
USSID .... United States Signals Intelligence
Directive
USSS .... United States SIGINT System

VHF .... very high frequency
VMAQ ....Marine tactical electronic warfare
squadron
VPN ....voice product net
VTC .... video teleconferencing

WAN.. wide area network

Section II

Definitions

A

all-source intelligence Intelligence products and/or organizations and activities that incorporate all sources of information, including, most frequently, human resources intelligence, imagery intelligence, measurement and signature intelligence, signals intelligence, and open source data, in the production of finished intelligence. (Join Pub 1-02)

amphibious objective area—A geographical area, delineated in the initiating directive, for purposes of command and control (C2) within which is located the objective(s) to be secured by the amphibious task force (ATF). This area must be of sufficient size to ensure accomplishment of the ATF's mission and must provide sufficient area for conducting necessary sea, air, and land operations. Also called **AOA**. (Joint Pub 1-02)

area of interest—That area of concern to the commander, including the area of influence, areas adjacent thereto, and extending into enemy territory to the objectives of current or planned operations. This area also includes areas occupied by enemy forces who could jeopardize the accomplishment of the mission. Also called **AOI**. (Joint Pub 1-02)

area of operations—An operational area defined by the joint force commander for land and naval forces. Areas of operation do not typically encompass the entire operational area of the joint force commander, but should be large enough for component commanders to accomplish their missions and protect their forces. Also called **AO**. (Joint Pub 1-02)

B

basic intelligence—Fundamental intelligence concerning the general situation, resources, capabilities, and vulnerabilities of foreign countries or areas which may be used as reference material in the planning of operations at any level and in evaluating subsequent information relating to the same subject. (Joint Pub 1-02)

battle damage assessment—The timely and accurate estimate of damage resulting from the application of military force, either lethal or nonlethal, against a predetermined objective. Battle damage assessment can be applied to the employment of all types of weapon systems (air, ground, naval, and special forces weapon systems) throughout the range of military operations. Battle damage assessment is primarily an intelligence responsibility with required inputs and coordination from the operators. Battle damage assessment is composed of physical damage assessment, functional damage assessment, and target system assessment. Also called **BDA**. (Joint Pub 1-02) In Marine Corps usage, the timely and accurate estimate of the damage resulting from the application of military force. BDA estimates physical damage to a particular target, functional damage to that target, and the capability of the entire target system to continue its operations. (MCRP 5-12C)

battlespace—All aspects of air, surface, subsurface, land, space, and electromagnetic spectru which encompass the area of influence and area of interest. (MCRP 5-12C)

battlespace dominance—The degree of control over the dimensions of the battlespace which enhances friendly freedom of action and denies enemy freedom of action. It permits force sustainment and application of power projection to accomplish the full range of potential operational and tactical missions. It includes all actions conducted against enemy capabilities to influence future operations. (MCRP 5-12C)

C

centralized control—In military operations, a mode of battlespace management in which one echelon of command exercises total authority and direction of all aspects of one or more warfighting functions. It is a method of control where detailed orders are issued and total unity of action is the overriding consideration. (MCRP 5-12C)

collection—In Marine Corps usage, the gathering of intelligence data and information to satisfy the identified requirements. (MCRP 5-12C)

collection management—The process of converting intelligence requirements into collection requirements, establishing priorities, tasking o coordinating with appropriate collection sources or agencies, monitoring results and retasking, as required. (Joint Pub 1-02) Its purpose is to conduct an effective effort to collect all necessary data while ensuring the efficient use of limited and valuable collection assets. (MCRP 2-1)

combat data—Data derived from reporting by operational units. (MCRP 5-12C)

combatant command—A unified or specified command with a broad continuing mission under a single commander established and so designated by the President through the Secretary of Defense and with the advice and assistance of Chairman of the Joint Chiefs of Staff. Combatant command typically have geographic or functional responsibilities. (Joint Pub 1-02)

command and control—The exercise of authority and direction by a properly designated commander over assigned and attached forces in the accomplishment of the mission. Command and control functions are performed through an arrangement of personnel, equipment, communications, facilities, and procedures employed by a commander in planning, directing, coordinating, and controlling forces and operations in the accomplishment of the mission. Also called **C2**. (Joint Pub 1-02) The means by which a commander recognizes what needs to be done and sees to it that appropriate actions are taken. (MCRP 5-12C)

command and control warfare—The integrated use of operations security, military deception, psychological operations, electronic warfare, and physical destruction, mutually supported by intel-

ligence, to deny information to, influence, degrade, or destroy adversary command and control capabilities, while protecting friendly command and control capabilities against such actions. Also called **C2W**. (Joint Pub 2-0)

commander's critical information requirements—Information regarding the enemy and friendly activities and the environment identified by the commander as critical to maintaining situational awareness, planning future activities, and facilitating timely decisionmaking. Also called **CCIR**. Note: CCIRs are normally divided into three primary subcategories: priority intelligence requirements, friendly force information requirements, and essential elements of friendly information. (MCRP 5-12C)

commander's intent—A commander's clear, concise articulation of the purpose(s) behind one or more tasks assigned to a subordinate. It is one of two parts of every mission statement which guides the exercise of initiative in the absence of instructions. (MCRP 5-12C)

communications intelligence—Technical and intelligence information derived from foreign communications by other than the intended recipients. Also called **COMINT**. (Joint Pub 1-02)

communications security—The protection resulting from all measures designed to deny unauthorized persons information of value which might be derived from the possession and study of telecommunications, or to mislead unauthorized persons in their interpretation of the results o such possession and study. Also called **COMSEC**. (Joint Pub 1-02 extract)

coordination—The action necessary to ensure adequately integrated relationships between separate organizations located in the same area. Coordination may include such matters as fire support, emergency defense measures, area intelligence and other situations in which coordination is considered necessary. (MCRP 5-12C)

critical information—Specific facts about friendly intentions, capabilities, and activities vitally needed by adversaries for them to plan and act effectively so as to guarantee failure or unacceptable consequences for friendly mission accomplishment. (Joint Pub 1-02)

critical intelligence—Intelligence which is crucial and requires the immediate attention of the commander. It is required to enable the commander to make decisions that will provide a timely and appropriate response to actions by the potential/ actual enemy. It includes but is not limited to the following: a. strong indications of the imminent outbreak of hostilities of any type (warning of attack); b. aggression of any nature against a friendly country; c. indications or use of nuclear-biological-chemical weapons (target); and d. significant events within potential enemy countries that may lead to modification of nuclear strike plans. (Joint Pub 1-02)

critical vulnerability—An aspect of a center of gravity that if exploited will do the most significant damage to an adversary's ability to resist. A vulnerability cannot be critical unless it undermines a key strength. Also called **CV**. (MCRP 5-12C)

D

decentralized control—In military operations, a mode of battlespace management in which a command echelon may delegate some or all authority and direction for warfighting functions to subordinates. It requires careful and clear articulation of mission, intent, and main effort to unify efforts of subordinate leaders. (MCRP 5-12C)

descriptive intelligence Class of intelligence which describes existing and previously existing conditions with the intent to promote situational awareness. Descriptive intelligence has two components: *basic intelligen* , which is general background knowledge about established and relatively constant conditions; and *current intelligence*, which is concerned with describing the existing situation. (MCRP 5-12C)

detachment—**1.** A part of a unit separated from its main organization for duty elsewhere. **2.** A temporary military or naval unit formed from other units or parts of units. (Joint Pub 1-02)

direction finding—A procedure for obtaining bearings of radio frequency emitters by using a highly directional antenna and a display unit on an intercept receive or ancillary equipment. (Joint Pub 1-02)

dissemination—Conveyance of intelligence to users in a suitable form. (Joint Pub 1-02)

E

electronic attack—That division of electronic warfare involving the use of electromagnetic, directed energy, or antiradiation weapons to attack personnel, facilities, or equipment with the intent of degrading, neutralizing, or destroying enemy combat capability. Also called **EA**. (Joint Pub 1-02)

electronic protection—That division of electronic warfare involving actions taken to protect personnel, facilities, and equipment from any effects of friendly or enemy employment of electronic warfare that degrade, neutralize, or destroy friendly combat capability. Also called **EP**. (Joint Pub 1-02)

electronic reconnaissance—The detection, identification, evaluation, and location of foreign electromagnetic radiations emanating from other than nuclear detonations or radioactive sources. (Joint Pub 1-02)

electronic warfare—Any military action involving the use of electromagnetic and directed energy to control the electromagnetic spectrum or to attack the enemy. Also called **EW**. The three major subdivisions within electronic warfare are **electronic attack, electronic protection**, and **electronic warfare support**. (Joint Pub 1-02)

electronic warfare support—That division of electronic warfare involving actions tasked by, or under direct control of, an operational commander to search for, intercept, identify, and locate sources of intentional and unintentional radiated electromagnetic energy for the purpose of immediate threat recognition. Thus, electronic warfare support provides information required for immediate decisions involving electronic warfare operations and other tactical actions such as threat avoidance, targeting, and homing. Also called **ES**. Electronic warfare support data can be used to produce signals intelligence (SIGINT), both communications intelligence (COMINT), and electronic intelligence (ELINT). (Joint Pub 1-02)

electronic intelligence—Technical and geolocation intelligence derived from foreign noncommunications electromagnetic radiations emanating from other than nuclear detonations or radioactive sources. Also called **ELINT**. (Joint Pub 1-02)

essential elements of friendly information—Key questions likely to be asked by adversary officials and intelligence systems about specific friendly intentions, capabilities, and activities, so they can obtain answers critical to their operational effectiveness. Also called **EEFI**. (Joint Pub 1-02) Specific facts about friendly intentions, capabilities, and activities needed by adversaries to plan and execute effective operations against our forces. (MCRP 5-12C)

estimative intelligence Class of intelligence which attempts to anticipate future possibilitie and probabilities based on an analysis of descriptive intelligence in the context of planned friendly and assessed enemy operations. (MCRP 5-12C)

F

friendly force information requirements—Information the commander needs about friendly forces in order to develop plans and make effective decisions. Depending upon the circumstances, information on unit location, composition readiness, personnel status, and logistics statu could become a friendly force information requirement. Also called **FFIR**. (MCRP 5-12C)

fusion—In intelligence usage, the process of examining all sources of intelligence and information to derive a complete assessment of activity. (Joint Pub 1-02)

G

global sourcing—A process of force provision or augmentation whereby resources may be drawn from any location/command worldwide. (MCRP 5-12C)

I

indications and warning—Those intelligenc activities intended to detect and report time-sensitive intelligence information on foreign developments that could involve a threat to the Unite States or allied military, political, or economic interests or to US citizens abroad. It includes forewarning of enemy actions or intentions; the imminence of hostilities; insurgency; nuclear/non-nuclear attack on the United States, its overseas forces, or allied nations; hostile reactions to United States reconnaissance activities; terrorists' attacks; and other similar events. Also called **I&W**. (Joint Pub 2-01)

intelligence—The product resulting from the collection, processing, integration, analysis, evaluation, and interpretation of evaluated information concerning foreign countries or areas. Information and knowledge about an adversary obtained through observation, investigation, analysis, o understanding. (Joint Pub 1-02) Also in Marine Corps usage, intelligence is knowledge about the enemy or the surrounding environment needed to support decisionmaking. This knowledge is the result of the collection, processing, exploitation, evaluation, integration, analysis, and interpretation of available information about the battlespace and threat. (MCRP 5-12C)

intelligence cycle—The process by which information is converted into intelligence and made available to users. (Joint Pub 2-01)

intelligence data—Data derived from assets primarily dedicated to intelligence collection such as imagery systems, electronic intercept equipment, human intelligence sources, etc. (MCRP 5-12C)

intelligence discipline—A well-defined area o intelligence collection, processing, exploitation and reporting using a specific category of technical or human resources. There are five major disciplines: human intelligence, imagery intelligence, measurement and signature intelligence, signals intelligence (communications intelligence, electronic intelligence, and foreign instrumentation signals intelligence), and open source intelligence. (Joint Pub 1-02)

intelligence operations—The variety of intelligence tasks that are carried out by various intelligence organizations and activities. (Joint Pub 1-02 extract)

intelligence preparation of the battlespace—An analytical methodology employed to reduce uncertainties concerning the enemy, environment, and terrain for all types of operations. Intelligence preparation of the battlespace builds an extensive data base for each potential area in which a unit may be required to operate. The data base is then analyzed in detail to determine the impact of the enemy, environment, and terrain on operation and presents it in graphic form. Intelligence preparation of the battlespace is a continuing process. Also called **IPB**. (Joint Pub 1-02) In Marine Corps usage, the systematic, continuous process of analyzing the threat and environment in a specific geographic area. (MCRP 5-12C)

intelligence requirement—1. Any subject, general or specific, upon which there is a need for the collection of information or the production of intelligence. (Joint Pub 1-02 2. In Marine Corps usage, questions about the enemy and the environment, the answers to which a commander requires to make sound decisions. Also called **IR**. (MCRP 5-12C)

J

joint deployable intelligence support system—A transportable workstation and communications suite that electronically extends a joint intelligence center to a joint task force or other tactical user. Also called **JDISS**. (Joint Pub 1-02)

joint force—A general term applied to a force composed of significant elements, assigned or attached, of two or more Military Departments, operating under a single joint force commander. (Joint Pub 1-02)

joint intelligence center—The intelligence center of the joint force headquarters. The joint intelligence center is responsible for providing and producing the intelligence required to support the joint force commander and staff, components, task forces and elements, and the national intelligence community. Also called **JIC**. (Joint Pub 1-02)

Joint Worldwide Intelligence Communications System—The sensitive compartmented information portion of the Defense Information System Network. It incorporates advanced networking technologies that permit point-to-poin or multipoint information exchange involving voice, text, graphics, data, and video teleconferencing. Also called **JWICS**. (Joint Pub 1-02)

M

main effort—The designated subordinate unit whose mission at a given point in time is mos critical to overall mission success. It is usually weighted with the preponderance of combat power and is directed against a center of gravity through a critical vulnerability. (MCRP 5-12C)

maneuver warfare—A warfighting philosophy that seeks to shatter the enemy's cohesion through a variety of rapid, focused, and unexpected actions which create a turbulent and rapidly deteriorating situation with which the enemy cannot cope. (MCRP 5-12C)

Marine Corps Planning Process—A six-step methodology which helps organize the though processes of the commander and staff throughout the planning and execution of military operations. It focuses on the threat and is based on the Marine Corps philosophy of maneuver warfare. It capitalizes on the principle of unity of command and supports the establishment and maintenance o tempo. The six steps consist of mission analysis, course of action development, course of action analysis, comparison/decision, orders development, and transition. Also called **MCPP**. Note: Tenets of the MCPP include top down planning, single battle concept, and integrated planning (MCRP 5-12C)

N

named area of interest—A point or area along a particular avenue of approach through which enemy activity is expected to occur. Activity or lack of activity within a named area of interest will help to confirm or deny a particular enemy course of action. Also called **NAI**. (MCRP 5-12C)

national intelligence support team—A nationally sourced team composed of intelligence and communications experts from either Defense Intelligence Agency, Central Intelligence Agency, National Security Agency, or any combination of these agencies. Also called **NIST**. (Joint Pub 2-01)

O

operational architecture—A description (often graphical) of the operational elements, assigned tasks, and information flows required to support the warfighter. It defines the type of information, the frequency of exchange, and what tasks are supported by these information exchanges. Also called **OA**. (MCRP 5-12C)

operational control—Transferable command authority that may be exercised by commanders a any echelon at or below the level of combatan command. Operational control is inherent in combatant command (command authority). Operational control may be delegated and is the authority to perform those functions of command over subordinate forces involving organizing and employing commands and forces, assigning tasks, designating objectives, and giving authoritative direction necessary to accomplish the mission. Operational control includes authoritative direction over all aspects of military operations and joint training necessary to accomplish mission assigned to the command. Operational control should be exercised through the commanders o subordinate organizations. Normally this authority is exercised through subordinate joint force commanders and Service and/or functional component commanders. Operational control normally provides full authority to organize commands and forces and to employ those forces as the commander in operational control considers necessary to accomplish assigned missions. Operational control does not, in and of itself, include authoritative direction for logistics or matters of administration, discipline, internal organization, or un training. Also called **OPCON**. (Joint Pub 1-02)

operations control and analysis center—Main node for the command and control of radio battalion signals intelligence operations and the overall coordination of MAGTF signals intelligence operations. Processes, analyzes, produces, and disseminates signals intelligence-derived information and directs the ground-based electronic warfare activities of the radio battalion. Also called **OCAC**. (MCRP 5-12C)

order of battle—The identification, strength, command structure, and disposition of the personnel, units, and equipment of any military force Also called **OOB**. (Joint Pub 1-02)

P

priority intelligence requirements—**1.** Those intelligence requirements for which a commander has an anticipated and stated priority in his task of planning and decisionmaking. Also called **PIR**. (Joint Pub 1-02) **2.** In Marine Corps usage, an intelligence requirement associated with a decision that will critically affect the overall success of the command's mission. (MCRP 5-12C)

production management—Encompasses determining the scope, content, and format of each intelligence product, developing a plan and schedule for the development of each product, assigning priorities among the various production requirements, allocating processing, exploitation, and production resources, and integrating production efforts with intelligence collection and dissemination. (MCRP 5-12C)

R

reach back—The ability to exploit resources, capabilities, expertise, etc., not physically located in the theater or a joint operations area, when established. (MCRP 5-12C)

S

sensitive compartmented information All information and materials bearing special community controls indicating restricted handling within present and future community intelligence collection programs and their end products for which community systems of compartmentation have been or will be formally established. (These controls are over and above the provisions of DOD 52001R, Information Security Program Regulation.) Also called **SCI**. (Joint Pub 1-02)

sensitive compartmented information facility—An accredited area, room, group of rooms, or installation where sensitive compartmented information may be stored, used, discussed, and/or electronically processed. SCIF procedural and physical measures prevent the free access of persons unless they have been formally indoctrinated for the particular SCI authorized for use or storage within the SCIF. Also called **SCIF**. See also **sensitive compartmented information**. (Joint Pub 1-02)

sensor data—Data derived from sensors whose primary mission is surveillance or target acquisition, such as air surveillance radars, counterbattery radars, and remote ground sensors. (MCR 5-12C)

Service component command—A command consisting of the Service component commander and all those Service forces such as individuals units, detachments, organizations, and installations under the command, including the support forces that have been assigned to a combatant command, or further assigned to a subordinate unified command or joint task force. (Joint Pub 1-02)

signals intelligence—A category of intelligence comprising either individually or in combination all communications intelligence, electronic intelligence, and foreign instrumentation signals intelligence, however transmitted. Also called **SIGINT**. (Joint Pub 1-02)

SIGINT operational tasking authority—A military commanders's authority, delegated by DIRNSA/CHCSS, to operationally direct and levy SIGINT requirements on designated SIGINT resources. This includes authority to deploy and redeploy all or part of the SIGINT resources for which SOTA has been delegated. Also called **SOTA**. (USSID 1, *SIGINT Operating Policy*)

situational awareness—Knowledge and understanding of the current situation which promotes timely, relevant and accurate assessment of friendly, enemy, and other operations within the battlespace in order to facilitate decisionmaking. An informational perspective and skill that foster an ability to determine quickly the context and relevance of events that are unfolding. (MCRP 5-12C)

split base—Two or more portions of the same force conducting or supporting operations fro separate physical locations. (MCRP 5-12C)

surveillance and reconnaissance center—Primary element responsible for the supervision o MAGTF intelligence collection operations. Directs, coordinates, and monitors intelligence collection operations conducted by organic, attached, and direct support collection assets. Also called **SARC**. (MCRP 5-12C)

sustained operations ashore—The employment of Marine Corps forces on land for an extended duration. It can occur with or without sustainment from the sea. Also called **SOA**. (MCRP 5-12C)

systems architecture—Defines the physical connection, location, and identification of key nodes, circuits, networks, warfighting platforms, etc and specific system and component performance parameters. The systems architecture is constructed to satisfy operational architecture requirements per standards defined in the technical architecture. The systems architecture shows how multiple systems within a subject area link and interoperate and may describe the internal construction or operations of particular systems within the architecture. Also called **SA**. (MCRP 5-12C)

T

tactical intelligence—Intelligence that is required for planning and conducting tactical operations. (Joint Pub 1-02) In Marine Corps usage, tactical intelligence is concerned primarily with the location, capabilities, and possible intentions of enemy units on the battlefield and with the tactical aspects of terrain and weather within the battlespace. (MCRP 5-12C)

technical architecture—The technical architecture identifies the services, interfaces, standards, and their relationships. It provides the technica guidelines for implementation of systems upon which engineering specifications are based, common building blocks are built, and product line are developed. Also called **TA**. (MCRP 5-12C)

technical control—The performance of specialized or professional service, or the exercise o professional guidance or direction through the establishment of policies and procedures.

tempo—The relative speed and rhythm of military operations over time. (MCRP 5-12C)

W

warfighting functions—The six mutually supporting military activities integrated in the conduct of all military operations are:

1. command and control—The means by which a commander recognizes what needs to be done and sees to it that appropriate actions are taken.

2. maneuver—The movement of forces for the purpose of gaining an advantage over the enemy.

3. fires—Those means used to delay, disrupt, degrade, or destroy enemy capabilities, forces, or facilities as well as affect the enemy's will to fight.

4. intelligence—Knowledge about the enemy or the surrounding environment needed to support decisionmaking.

5. logistics—All activities required to move and sustain military forces.

6. force protection—Actions or efforts used to safeguard own centers of gravity while protecting, concealing, reducing, or eliminating friendly critical vulnerabilities.

Also called **WF**. (MCRP 5-12C)

Appendix G

References and Related Publications

Department of Defense Directives (DODDs)

S-3115.7	Signals Intelligence
5105.21-M-1	Sensitive Compartmented Information (SCI) Security Manual, Administrative Security
TS-5105.21-M-2	Sensitive Compartmented Information (SCI) Security Manual, Communications Intelligence (COMINT) Policy
TS- 5105.21-M-3	Sensitive Compartmented Information (SCI) Security Manual, TK Policy
5200.1	DOD Information Security Program
5210.70	DOD Cryptologic Training

Director of Central Intelligence Directives (DCIDs)

1/14	Personnel Security Standards and Procedures Governing Eligibility for Access to Sensitive Compartmented Information
1/16	Security Manual for Uniform Protection of Intelligence Processed in AISs and Networks
1/21	Physical Security Standards for Sensitive Compartmented Information Facilities

United States Signals Intelligence Directive (USSIDs)

1	SIGINT Operating Policy
4	Concept of SIGINT Support to Military Commanders
56	Exercise SIGINT
200	Technical SIGINT Reporting
240	ELINT Processing, Analysis, Reporting, and Forwarding Procedures
300	SIGINT Reporting
316	Non-Codeword Reporting Program
340	Tactical ELINT Reporting
341	Technical ELINT Reporting
510	Information for SIGINT Users

Defense Intelligence Agency Manual (DIAM)

50-4	Department of Defense Intelligence Information Systems (DODIIS) Information Security (INFOSEC) Program

Department of the Navy Supplement (NAVSUP) to DODD

5105.21-M-1   SCI Administrative Security Manual

Joint Publications (Joint Pubs)

1-02   Department of Defense Dictionary of Military and
              Associated Terms
2-0   Doctrine for Intelligence Support to Joint Operations
2-01   Joint Intelligence Support to Military Operations
2-02   National Intelligence Support to Joint Operations
3-02   Joint Doctrine for Amphibious Operations
3-13.1   Joint Doctrine for Command and Control Warfare
3-54   Joint Doctrine for Operations Security
5-0   Doctrine for Planning Joint Operations
6-0   Doctrine for C4 Systems Support to Joint Operations

Marine Corps Doctrinal Publications (MCDPs)

1   Warfighting
2   Intelligence
3   Expeditionary Operations
4   Logistics
5   Planning
6   Command and Control

Marine Corps Warfighting Publications (MCWPs)

2-1   Intelligence Operations
6-22   Communications and Information Systems

Marine Corps Reference Publication (MCRP)

5-12C   Marine Corps Supplement to the Department of
              Defense Dictionary of Military and
              Associated Terms
5-12D   Organization of Marine Corps Forces

Marine Corps Orders (MCOs)

1510.50A   Individual Training Standard (ITS) System for the
              Signals Intelligence/Ground Electronic Warfare
              Occupational Field (OccFld) 26
5500.6F   Arming of Security and Law Enforcement (LE)
              Personnel and the Use of Force

Army Field Manuals (FMs)

34-2	Collection Management and Synchronization Planning
34-130	Intelligence Preparation of the Battlefield

Related Publication

Joint Tactical Exploitation of National Systems (J-TENS) Manual

www.ingramcontent.com/pod-product-compliance
Lightning Source LLC
Chambersburg PA
CBHW082243310526
45795CB00013B/2017